CONTENTS

Stereotyping in Literature – The Annuals Example

A Little Book of Big Questions

(Philosophical talking points)

By Greg Tuck

WHAT SORT OF SOCIETY SHOULD WE LIVE IN?

Humans have grown beyond the simple basic necessities to develop a social structure. There are four main pillars that support any society. Simply put they are: leadership or governance, education, justice and equity. Failure in one or more of these can lead to social tension and upheaval. The difficulty is getting the balance right given the inherent nature of different individual wants and needs. We strive towards a utopian existence but are held back by our often dystopian attitude towards others.

There have been so many attempts to draft the perfect societal structure but the one main factor all have not taken into account is the fact that we are dealing with human beings. Humans are competitive, greedy and selfish. Team work is not an inbuilt part of human DNA. It needs to be taught. So does selflessness. These two aspects would help to unite people so that a long-lasting society could be developed and not be held together by force and oppression.

Leadership/governance

As in many of the more primitive tribes, there are two seats of power. One is the leader of the tribe and the other is the spiritual adviser/witch doctor. Little has changed in the so called more civilized societies. In some it is less obvious. In some the religion may be the worship of money but it all works the same. There is governance and there is marketing of that governance otherwise known as propaganda. Governance is all about establish laws for the society but often those laws are there to maintain those leading in that role. The marketing of the governance is done through religion and education and again these are used to maintain those leading in that role. In hindsight the rise and rule of Hitler was the most blatant use of that. He used his diatribes and the Propaganda Ministry to conform people to his beliefs. He used laws and the heavy enforcement of those laws to suppress any opposition to those beliefs. Then he set out to conquer the world and get others to follow his dogma at any price. It is a practice that had been used in the past but never to such an extent.

So which ism is the best? Capitalism promotes scientific development and improvement in material things. Communism in its purest form has some of the essential structures that provide a working and workable society but the practical application of it is always riddled with corruption. Socialism, which falls somewhere between the two, is a compromise that leaves out the best of both, but retains the worst of both. For the past century there has been the push for democracy, the one person one vote system but the governments elected by this are just as open to corruption as any other. The equal vote is a fallacy anyway. Party politics ends up making a mockery of it in many nations. The propaganda prior to an election leaves many voters unsure of what and who they are voting for. The voters themselves bring to the table all their own prejudices and self-interest and that can taint the election process as they may not be looking at what is best for society as a whole. Those elected do not need to follow the wishes of their electorate once elected and can push their own wheelbarrows and agendas as they see fit. If voters were better educated in what could and should be, then there may be a chance of true democracy. Currently it is a falsehood, yet one that democratic countries will wage war upon others for. If there is a dictatorship, even a benevolent one, many democratic nations will find reasons to intervene or invade and thrust their form of governance on that country, especially if there is monetary gain in it.

The issue of adversarial government is often raised. Advocates of it say that it increases debate and thus better outcomes are gained. In practice that is not always the case. In essence it means that the notion of winning and losing comes to the fore. This plays into the hands of those seeking power rather than ways of benefitting society itself. It doesn't encourage consensus of all who may be elected, but pits teams against each other. It plays to the baser instincts of mankind. Some nations have more civilized debates but the outcome is much the same as those that don't. Generally, the community suffers through inaction, slow decision making, horse-trading and corruption. Ideology often stymies practical solutions.

Education

Education has been suggested as the means of breaking out of poverty and rising up the totem pole of society. However, privilege breeds privilege in society and those who have higher bank balances can buy better education for their children because education too is a commodity that has a price. Children from poorer areas attend factor in what was in effect a power struggle. Little has changed in the Middle East today, but the underlying reason for the unrest is no longer just a desire for land that is more fertile but the wealth that goes with the mineral rights for the land. Religious bodies would be far less antagonistic if they looked at what different religions had in common, not what they don't.

Justice

There is a tendency to associate the word justice with the word law. Laws are an important structure that provide parameters for human behaviour. But justice is determined by the acceptance by the populace that fairness is at the heart of the laws. In different tribes, states and nations, laws are also very different. No-one has got them right. Importing or imposing a set of laws doesn't work because the community does not own them, feels they have not had a say in developing them and will rebel against them. The enforcement of those imposed laws is almost certain to initiate conflict. Laws do need to be enforced equally and fairly. Justice needs to be kept separate from government. Policing of the laws needs to be kept separate from the other two. Without this separation of powers, faith in the justice system will quickly be lost. Laws need to be challenged to prove they are needed and are just. However, the means of challenging those laws needs to be an inbuilt part of the justice system or that system will ultimately fail.

One of the sad traits of humans is that for most of their lives many believe that they are the centre of the universe. They cannot see the bigger picture. What would be fair and just for someone else would be an abhorrence if applied to themselves. The idea that one law applies to all is important but just as important is that one punishment should not always apply to all. Each breach of the law should be judged on its merits because each circumstance is different. Privilege or wealth should not be able to buy you a better outcome. Such actions will drive a lack of faith in the legal system. That fact that those who peddle their wares as legal advocates and make grossly disproportionate income for their advice is a sad indictment on a legal system that has made itself too complicated for the good of the bulk of society.

Equality

Humans need to know that they have a role and that what they do is valued by others. This gives a sense of purpose. Many so-called lesser creatures already have those things in place and their society is not built like a house of cards as human society is. The need for power, status and wealth has gradually increased since the dawn of mankind and they have beleaguered almost all societies over time. The notion that everyone is created equally, has equal opportunities and play an equal part in society is a myth that is pedalled by those in a higher station wanting to cement their power base. It is an idyll that is used to both calm and stir the masses. Simply by paying people different wages and making life more difficult for those in need displays this. Those who sweep gutters are held in more disdain than those who cure the ill. Yet both are important to make a functioning society. We embed social differences though wealth and we entrench them through laws which favour those higher up the pecking order.

In a capitalist society there is a material driven approach in play. Commodities owned by individuals are a measure of their worth and have become the status symbol. Yet so few of the very wealthy make real contributions back into the society that has allowed them the sort of lifestyle they lead. They have the money to find ways to rort tax systems so that they can retain their wealth. Even their charitable donations are used to curb the impact tax has on their accumulated wealth. Wages and income are not in-line with the real contributions that individuals make to a society in a capitalistic world. However, the notion that everyone should be paid the same wage is decried because it would not encourage growth of an economy and only encourage sloth and dependency. Entrenched in most people's upbringing is the knowledge that certain occupations are of far less importance than others. Yet are they in reality? Why is a teacher or a nurse held in much lower esteem than a stockbroker who merely gambles on future profits of companies? The answer to the latter is that has been the status quo for such a long time and it suits those higher up the social scale to keep it that way.

The argument can be made that society now has a safety net for those who are in need. It wasn't always so but does the safety net go far enough? Homelessness is on the increase in first world countries despite rises in gross domestic product. The reason is these societies' profiles encourage the rich to get richer and the divide between the poor and rich to expand. In many poorer countries there is no safety net. The poor are deemed not worth saving. In a twenty first century world of globalisation, poorer people have become more expendable on a wider basis. Richer nations, multinationals and individuals see those less well off as further victims to exploit. There is enough wealth of food, water and money to look after everyone in the world, but there is not enough wealth of compassion, understanding and humanity to do that. What many in society would see as necessary services and items to survive in today's world are not egalitarian or universally obtainable.

In the past revolutions have begun because of the inequality that is perceived by the majority. Some have been peaceful and others have been devastating. Hitler only came to power because Germany was plunged into destitution because they lost the First World War. France's famous revolution was a case of the rich wanting to have the cake and eat it to, leaving the peasants hungry. The demise of apartheid in South Africa was far more peaceful but nevertheless for the same reasons. Major flare ups around the world have the same underlying issues: a feeling of inequality that challenges the status quo; a feeling of being undervalued by those who seem to have everything including the power to make things better.

In the health system, as in the education system, money talks. Housing, access to transport and communication, recreational facilities and secure employment and thus food on the table are inextricably linked to money and status. As mentioned before, the legal system is also another perfect example of this. Money buys you a better legal team and you more often than not get a better outcome.

So, in a better society would it be better to have government, judiciary, religion and education all in step with each other? Given Hitler combined them all to such a devastating effect perhaps it would be wise to learn from the past and keep them as separate as possible.

WHY DON'T PEOPLE THINK LIKE I DO?

We have enough wealth throughout the world that no one needs to live in poverty, so why do we spend it on armaments and defence? We seem to want to keep what we have and not lose our own materialistic belonging as we try to gain more. Why is there a cultural divide between rich and poor? We have created the need to own land to determine our status in society. How much wealth is enough anyway? Nowadays we believe that wealth and the value of a person are determined solely by material possessions and bank balances, and that is how they are remembered after they have passed away. What they leave behind as a legacy should be more than just what is distributed to their heirs in terms of money.

Why do people commit crimes that are blatantly wrong by normal society standards? I'm not talking about those who don't know or understand right from wrong, but those who do and choose to commit crimes. Genocide, murder and executions are committed by societies and individuals simply because life is an expendable item. It is for some the solving of a problem, others a religious or national doctrine and somehow for others it has become a pleasurable experience. At times there seems no sanctity of human life, no value put on it. We condone theft that is white collar crime. For years assault in the home has been labelled as domestic violence and been accepted. Historically religious bodies have been above the law. No taxes are paid and what otherwise would be criminal cases in lay society are hushed up, covered up and dealt with by religious authorities.

Why do we choose as leaders of our nations some of the least capable of leading and some who will lead us down the wrong path? War and the decimation of cultures have been proven to be so damaging to human civilization over centuries, yet we learn nothing from history. Our elected leaders seem all too ready and gung-ho to play the child like bully and claim we have to defend ourselves often by attacking those who are least capable of defending themselves. They lead from the rear and send our young out, often to sacrifice their lives without knowing why. Are people too disinterested, feeling too powerless and disenfranchised to make better choices for leadership? Are they too involved in their own lives? Are they too busy living on a hand to mouth existence?

Why do laws and religious and cultural practices determine who is a fit and proper person within our society? Throughout history discrimination has led to rebellion, uprisings and war. Are some people created more equal than others? It seems everyone gets a turn to be discriminated against and many have lots of turns. Women, indigenous people, those of different colour race or creed, non-heterosexuals, the poor, the young, the old…. where is the logic in that? To create a feeling of our own importance, humans find someone else to denigrate.

Why do babies and children die? What sins have they committed? Are they being punished for other people's sins? We have across the world enough scientific understanding, knowledge and capacity to alleviate many of the childhood illnesses and exposure to famine, yet we choose not to share because there is no financial gain for us, or are told that it is not in our best interests. Companies rape and plunder the wealth of smaller nations for their own gain, leaving behind civil unrest and a population that is barely above subsistence level. We turn a blind eye to this looting because it is done by legitimate businesses who show little compassion for those that are left in poverty, particularly children. With that poverty, often comes disease, malnutrition and the whole thing becomes a downward spiral.

Why are people being denied an open minded, secular education that encourages the asking of questions and one that does not instil just answers that blatant propaganda and lies? Controlling what people hear and see, learn and think, seems to be an obsession for those who have the power to do it. It reaffirms their own destiny, but pays little credence to the separate and possible potential of those that are being taught. Many of the young merely become clones of or subservient to their elders simply because they know no different. Their ignorance is bliss for those seeking control. National pride can become fanaticism. Religious observance can become zealotry.

Humans are supposedly the most intelligent of all species, yet why do we fail to heed the warnings that they are in fact destroying the planet that sustains our existence? Whilst human involvement in climate change has been proven beyond just a radical theory, the vast populace kowtow to the might of big business and out of touch leaders who seem averse to recognising the bleeding obvious. There is only short term thinking by these people who believe that their career and profit make everything else insubstantial. When they are proven wrong, they will have retired, died or made enough money from their corporate greed not to have to worry.

Why do so few very good leaders come along? Or maybe a better question would be, why do so very few good leaders come to the fore? Historically the majority of leaders have been male and that masculinity has been a driving force. As pack animals, humans turn to the alpha male who in most cases wants to dominate his own and other packs. Given a change in circumstances with the rise in feminism, it will be interesting to see how emerging female leaders shape the future of nations. There have been too few Nelson Mandela's, Mahatma Gandhi's, Martin Luther King's and Tenzin Gyatso (Dalai Lama)'s throughout history. In religion the wisest leaders such as Buddha, Confucius, Muhammad, Krishna, Martin Luther and Jesus of Nazareth have had their words twisted and teachings besmirched by those who have come after them. We have allowed the religious doctrines to become tainted and have acquiesced to those who would suppress great leaders.

If there is a god, why doesn't he/she/it intervene? Surely with a simple subtle alteration, leaders can be modified to take a less selfish, more open, kind, humane and sharing path. Or has god decided that we have made this bed and we have to lie in it. Are we just lab rats in some sort of labyrinth? Is this just an experiment that is going horribly wrong? Humans are tragically human and will never master the intricacies of dealing with each other to create and maintain a sustainable world where everyone is equal and working towards a common shared goal. So, if no superior being intervenes, how long do we have before we tear each other or the world apart?

WHAT CAN WE LEARN FROM DEATH?

There are two simple facts that can't be disputed. We are born. We die. In the infinite time of our universe we are a brief zeptosecond if indeed that. We as a species, so called of the higher order, don't dispute that; however, since earliest of times we have created cultures, traditions, religions and treatises to explain away death. We are plagued with notions of our life being carried on in a different form, of our life have a higher purpose, of a life that is well lived according to prescribed morals and ethics, being rewarded. Yet the facts remain, we are born, we die.

In the animal kingdom, the loss of life is mourned briefly and then it is time to move on. The need to survive takes over. Animals need to drink and eat and avoid being eaten. There is no time for soul searching. Man, as a species has too much time on his hands, too much time to think and too much time to provide reasons why dying is unacceptable in its actual form. We avoid reality in ways that animals don't. So, are we in fact a higher order species?

This fear of death, born through our basic fight or flight make up has been extrapolated allowing others to control and exploit our everyday lives. We are a social animal and our society has become so large and diverse that the death of one individual no longer seems to affect us, unless we have had some direct contact with them, or they have had an influence on our lives. Family and celebrities come to mind and we mourn them but strangers, particularly those who die in vast numbers have much less of an impact. If we wept and felt sympathy for all those who die, our lives would be so filled with remorse we would be unable to function. It is what allows rulers and warmongers to send others off to fight with little or no concern for those people's lives. The only lives that matter are often their own and those of their immediate family; and in some cases, not even the latter.

It is god's will when someone dies. God has called that person to him. That is what we have been told. What sort of god allows the death of a child who has barely had time to live? Is it the same god that doesn't interfere when some potentially catastrophic but preventable situation arises? We ascribe super powers to stop us believing in the actual truth that we start dying the day we are born. Some people live longer than others. There is no preordained date of one's death, unless we are born with a congenital abnormality. Even then some challenge and actually alter that prescribed scientific occurrence. Science is not exact. Religion is far less so.

Do we credit the extension in the longevity of human life to some god's work or to the advent of scientific development? If a person is able to exist longer on life support, hovering between life and death, more dead than alive is that at some god's intervention. We have long held the notion that euthanasia, suicide and assisted suicide is wrong according to the natural (and religious) order of things yet we have the counter idea when it comes to making sure that animals don't suffer unduly. Religion has long been the escape clause when it comes to people being permitted to decide their own fate.

Unbearable pain is something that humans have been forced to endure because of religious attitudes towards death. The weight of public opinion has for many years been unable to sway our lawmakers who have followed their own religious doctrine and refused to accept that death is something that needs to be acknowledged and dealt with in compassionate and secular terms. Doctors too have been caught up in a similar bind. They have been restricted by the tenet "first, do no harm". That has been taken as that a life must be saved at any cost and that death is harmful. Death is natural and is a consequence of living. In fact, they may actually do more harm by taking an unnatural approach.

Thus, quality of life and therefore of death must come under scrutiny. How do you measure such quality? Philosophical questions come to bear. Do we merely just exist? Is the quality of life determined by the morality and ethics we live by? Is everybody's definition of quality individually diverse? The church and the state would have us think differently. They impose upon us norms. In modern society celebrity role models are beginning to make more headway than in the past and even more than religious bodies in some cases. The "me-ness" of today's population, as exemplified particularly by social media, shows that individuals want to be seen, heard and noticed. We will be fed as false an impression about the quality of life by technology, as that gained from the religious and cultural sanctions in the past.

It all comes back to the inevitability of death. Life does not have to measured in fixed time units. Some people will live longer than others. That is just the way it is. It is what you do between birth and death that matters. That is the real measurement. For many who have a choice, they would rather do exciting, adventurous and outlandish things knowing the consequence is having a slightly briefer life than others who have opted to lead a dour existence. Life is not a longevity race. It isn't a last person standing affair where the prize is immortality. If death teaches us anything, it is that we are all mortal and that life is to be treasured, not measured.

Some people live their lives vicariously and most view their deaths vicariously. As a society we do not embrace death as a reality and so we allow others to determine what it actually is. From film-makers, to story writers, from scientists to priests, we have death placed in front of us but we fail to understand the concept. So many in the past have turned to religion to explain it and as science has progressed so many have turned slowly towards a more scientific interpretation. Just which is right? As any religious zealot or sardonic character will tell you, "God only knows!" However, until we begin to accept death as a part of life, rather than believing that it is something that happens to other people and not to me, we will have difficulty dealing with it when it comes.

Some people seem bent on hastening their own demise simply by their own lifestyle choices. Those in less fortunate social and financial situations may actually have less choice and less ability to prolong their lives. They can be seen to have far less quality in their lives. But is that so? Would it be far more correct that they make the most of every precious second that they are alive and those of us who are luckier, tend to waste far more. Those who are disabled, those who eke out a day to day existence, those who are challenged by life itself, probably know more about life than the rest of us.

People who accumulate a lot of wealth and material possessions during their lifetime face the same end as those who don't. When their time comes, it comes. They may have been able to prolong their lives more than others but they have only delayed the inevitable. Science can only do so much. Our bodies have a use by date and there is a planned obsolescence that makes a warranty worthless. We have been programmed to die. Delaying or denying that departure date won't alter the fact. We have a strange way of dealing with death. We go through rituals of mourning which amplify our own fears of death. Instead of celebrating a life, we focus on the empty space that someone leaves behind. In that way, we are very selfish.

In our time of mourning and grieving we are very susceptible to exploitation. The funeral business thrives, churches seek bequests and distant relatives seek a piece of the pie that has been left behind. We are made to feel that a box, in a tiny plot, with a lump of stone above, all of which are exorbitantly priced, is what our loved one would have wanted and the best way to provide a lasting memory of them. We are convinced that someone in robes is the best person to speak on behalf of a relative and to celebrate his or her life and indeed pass judgement on them. We are told by law that despite the wishes expressed in a will that the assets left behind may be challenged by those whom the dead person may have not known or wanted to have anything to do with. This takes place because we choose through tradition and ignorance not to look at what joy the person brought to us in life, but instead the lack of joy we will no longer receive from them. Our focus has been deliberately misaligned.

Death happens to us all. It is the one thing we have in common, yet it is the one thing that we choose not to contemplate and talk about.

WHAT IS LOVE?

What is "love"? It is the age-old question with no real answer. Everyone has a different interpretation and indeed that interpretation for every individual changes over time. A baby, a young child, a teenager, view parents and the love they share differently. Parents also change in the forms of love that they offer to their child and indeed between their children. Often the love shown is a reaction to what has been shown to them by their parents. Platonic love for a friend, sexual love for a partner, filial love for a relative all come under the broad banner of love and many of us experience all three in some way or form. However, the one that we tend to focus on the most is a combination of platonic and sexual love as we seek out a lifelong partner.

We have been bombarded with images, stories, poems and pictures of true love between people. The ones where fireworks explode, the earth moves, bluebirds sing and everything has a rosy tint to it. We are shaped by all of this and there is a common misunderstanding that it will happen to each of us one day. Books, paintings, photos and movie tickets are sold on that very premise. Dating agencies are set up hoping to ensnare as many people with the false advertising they promote. We are sold on the notion that somewhere, someone absolutely perfect for you is just waiting.

What are the chances of meeting the perfect person to spend your whole life with? Infinitesimal at best, is probably the right answer. Mathematically the odds are well and truly stacked against you.

Given that every individual has different wants, needs and desires, there is little chance of finding the Ms or Mr Right in the first place. There is no doubt, taking into account the billions of people in the world, someone, who is the perfect match is out there, but as for that person coming across your path at the time when you are both seeking a partner, well the odds are so remote as to be serendipitous. Hollywood would have us think otherwise of course.

Humans have been led to believe that love is a quantifiable object that these days a computer algorithm can resolve. Yet the vagaries of the human thought process and condition preclude any such matching. We change through experience and thus what the perfect partner requirements are, change daily or even more frequently than that. For any two people to match perfectly in space and time even for a short period without compromise is almost beyond the realms of possibility. There has to be a caveat on that because it can happen, so to say it would never happen, would be breaking the mathematical theoretical laws of probability.

For the most part, humans have been able, if only sometimes subconsciously, to look at realistic compromise to make relationships work. There has to be give and take. For some people they expect to continually take without having to give and thus are often the least successful in finding someone to share their lives with. There are also needy people who bend over backwards to ensure they stay in a relationship, but the quality of that relationship has to be called into question, especially if wants and desires are also factored in. Needs may be being met, but other factors that form the total package of love may have been set aside.

It begs the question as to whether love is all about negotiation and finding points of interest and commonality between two people. Is a skilled negotiator the one who can get the most out of a relationship? That depends on the level of compromise that he or she is also willing to show. Someone standing fast over major issues and conceding on less important ones at least is showing potential partners just the reality of the situation especially if done from the outset. The age-old maxim is correct. It is not how a person can change the other person but how willing they are to change themselves.

All this being said, much of the toing and froing takes place unspoken as couples get to know each other. The fact that it is not discussed can in some circumstances lead to misunderstandings and also to people going against their steadfast beliefs to try to retain a failing relationship. It would so much easier and efficient if people had barcodes that could be scanned so that prospective partners, could read between the lines and understand the nuances of the verbal and body language that a person they are interested in, is actually using. Some people would say that such an innovation would spoil the dating game and take the surprise and fun out of meeting new people. However, it may avoid the often frequently mixed messages and promises made that never get fulfilled.

How far does a person go to try to accommodate the desires of another person? That, in itself, is dependent on the attitudes of the individuals involved. How demanding a person is and how accommodating, don't have to be mutually exclusive. It is part of the argy bargy of finding a mutually agreeable middle road. Historically in a male/female relationship it has been the man's role to be the demanding one. Women were seen to be the chattels of the man and to achieve anything for themselves, they had to do subtle work arounds. This has a strong cultural and often religious links that in some societies persists today. A man was seen to be weak if he gave in to his partner's needs; and a woman conniving or rising above her station if she pushed her own agenda. In many societies that has begun to change as it precludes an equal partnership and an open conversation between partners. Whether the pendulum for some couples has swung a little bit too far the other way is anybody's guess.

Because the desire for a complete sexual and platonic relationship begins in puberty, for centuries parents have taken over the role of organising who their child should and can love. Teenagers are seeking their own boundaries at about the same time and parents who choose to overly interfere run a huge risk of losing the links with their child, particularly in this day and age. Their children are trying to break free and get a sense of their own independence and fail to realise that their parents went through the same situation when they were younger. Parents also seem to forget their youth and possible indiscretions that they experienced. For many it is a case of "Do what I say, not what I did!"

Possibly the greatest interference is the notion of arranged marriages. In the past, the nobility used these to forge military and court alliances. In commerce, such arrangements were used to sweeten deals and encourage mergers. Many cultures dictated that it was a parent's responsibility. The importance of a dowry given by the bride's parents influenced many of the choices. Whether there was love involved didn't matter. "They will learn to love, as we learned to love in marriages that were arranged for us." It sounds arcane and archaic but it too persists today. "They are young, what would they know? They will experiment and get it wrong." However, by insulating their children and confining them to what may be a lifelong loveless marriage, they may be denying their children a greater understanding of what love entails.

And historically the attitude towards homosexual love was horrific. Many were denied the opportunity to love someone simply because they were different to the norm. In many places it was a criminal act to even contemplate a homosexual relationship. Slowly these taboos are changing but not soon enough for many people who have had to endure a loveless life because they were different. Love also was denied to people who were in different social strata, followed different religions, were of a different ethnic background and so on. To many people it seemed that society, religion and culture was waging a war on love. The reality was entrenched prejudice was actually being further cemented in and the next generation would perpetuate the same practices. Science, particularly the development of the birth control pill which freed up women and gave them control over their own bodies, made dramatic changes. This was allied with the push for equality and education for all and soon major inroads into the restrictions placed on love by older generations and society's historical practices.

There is a danger if all social constraints are removed because all people prefer to have some boundaries to know where they are in space and time. The feedback is like a radar echo allowing us to better understand who we are and who others are around us. The radar ping for many of us is all about communicating with another person and finding out as much as we can before we decide to progress further down the continuum from accept through to love.

Tweets may have replaced love letters and Tinder swiping may have impacted the bar scene, but the desire to give and receive love hasn't changed that much. It is still as fragile. It still hurts when it falls over. In today's environment however, people can take it or leave it without the recriminations that once existed. People still fall in and out of love without fully understanding the complex nature of love. There exists a fear of failure but hopefully a sense of wonderment remains. The wonderment revolves around the interplay between two people. You can't love someone unless there is a similarly expressed feeling being received in return. If it isn't received and is unlikely to be received, then that "love" is merely is a mix of admiration and adoration and in its extremes is stalking!!!!

Love is as complex as the human mind. That is probably a good analogy because sometimes it feels like you have lost yours when you fall for someone. It is the greatest gift that you can bestow on another person. Though it costs nothing, it is priceless.

WHAT OF GOD?

God, if there is one, is often depicted as male and there may be good reason for that. Females are known to be in the main, more nurturing and supportive of the things that they have created. Males less so, although that is no hard and fast rule. Males like to experiment and move on. Perhaps that is what God has done with the Earth. He has thrown a few chemicals together in a test tube and then left what he created to see what happens. Perhaps, because he is immortal, so they say, and it only took six days to create the world, he went on to create other worlds elsewhere. He had a lot of time on his hands. Or maybe he just forgot. Males are notorious for forgetting. They become distracted easily and can only do one thing at a time. Maybe he was perhaps just ambivalent about what the outcome might be.

Nevertheless, we have what we have, a place to live on, a tiny speck in the universe where things keep reacting and evolving and dying out. There has been no intervention by God who is supposedly created man in his own image. The latter is most likely untrue. God is not human because there is no humanity in God. Something that permits famine, pestilence and plagues to occur and takes the lives of innocent children lacks humanity, so we should not assume that he is necessarily human. He is probably amorphous or merely a thought pattern and perhaps to some appears heartless as well.

Man has created the idea of there being a God to explain what he doesn't know or understand. The more mankind gains knowledge, the less the need to believe for many people. They are not swayed by archaic notions as put out by religious institutions which have failed to move with the times and come to a newer definition of what God is. The refinement of the definition needs to take place but is being held back by the same religious institutions that profess they know what the one true God is exactly like, even though they have little to back it up. They preach to the converted but those being converted become less and less each day.

Mankind has gone to war over beliefs in different versions of God or at least they have used that as an excuse. God has not intervened in these conflicts, to stop them or to support one side over another. Is that just a callous attitude or merely just an observational role he has taken on as part of the experiment? Is it a lack of compassion or a lack of omnipotence that has stopped God stepping in? As the tiny little figures on that speck of dust in the universe tear each other limb from limb, does it really matter in the big scheme of things? And it is a big scheme of things. Perhaps that is why nothing is done. God is too busy, even though he has all the time in the world, or universe in reality.

There have been many prophets and sons of God over the years and we have heard tales of miracles. The verification of these miracles is in itself an inexact science and as such the documentation and Chinese whisper folk tales that have started and at times ended religions will need to be continually re-examined as new technology is developed. There is no double jeopardy prevention here. Mankind has progressed by continually asking 'why?' and 'what if?'. To question is not necessarily a sign of doubt. It is also a way of seeking confirmation. Blind obedience is regressive and in the long run will decimate the numbers of believers.

Mankind seeks answers to the wonders around. Theories are conceived and tested, experiments are devised and then suppositions are made. Could man fly? What is beyond the Earth? How can something be done better? There have been no divine revelations that provide the answers and often the answers that have been created by mankind have unintended and disastrous results. Who would have thought that aeroplanes would become weapons of war and splitting the atom may end up destroying all of mankind? If God decreed that a certain fruit not be eaten, surely, he would have interceded to stop the theories that would destroy what he created or was it a case of 'hands off and see what transpires'. If it was the latter then such lack of compassion and foresight is enough to throw doubts as to the perfection of God.

Would it be better to say that we have no proof that there is no God or, would we be better off in believing in a God who is not omnipotent and all knowing? When we look at the natural beauty that surrounds us, feel the joy of a new born child, sense the inner strength and morality of the best of the human race, then there is a reason to believe that there is a higher power than us, but one who may not get everything right. No man could replicate nature, no man could instil the love of a parent and no man could readily explain why some people are closer to saints than others. Strands of DNA may go some way, but we are still at a loss as to explain all the minutiae that makes up our world and what triggers the random thoughts in the form of electrical impulses that cross the synapses of all creatures' brains. If these understandings were gained would we then be able to state that God doesn't exist? Probably not because there will always be more questions that have no answer and people will need to plug holes and the simplest way to do that apart from ignoring the questions entirely, is to have faith in something.

Faith is the driving force for most religions. It is what binds people together who are searching for answers beyond their comprehension. Like a reputation however it takes time to build up and seconds to destroy. A proven fact can be the destroyer and that is why religions to survive need to move with the times. Traditions may be well and good along with ceremonies and rituals but if beliefs remain lodged in the past then the religion itself withers and dies. The biggest hold that religions in the Middle Ages had over people was the control over knowledge. Withholding of education has been used as a tool by all sorts of bodies, the rich, the state, the powerful etc. to maintain control over the majority of the population. Detailed information was often withheld, distorted or debunked to maintain power. This is become so much harder in the technological world of today. There is a surfeit of knowledge but allied to that, it is hard to know what is fact and what is fiction.

Therein lies the dilemma for many people. Is God fact or fiction? Is there an afterlife or not? Most religions promise there is one and the more sceptical of us ask, "How do they know?" Atheists say there isn't and agnostics remain unsure. People of faith say that there has to be because what is the reason for living otherwise, as if a mortal life is some sort of proving ground. If it is a proving ground, who decides on the morality that is required to pass? Who has the right to pass judgement? Can God if God is not perfect? How can a day-old child who dies have had a chance to prove him or herself worthy of heaven? Do the social and economic circumstances come into play in any judgement? Different religions offer different versions of heaven or after-life? Which one is correct? You may have lived a perfectly acceptable life but been involved in the wrong religion and thus are excluded. Where do you go then? Some religions will put you in purgatory or limbo and some will cast you into hell.

These versions of heaven, purgatory and hell too have changed over the years as have some of the rules that determine where your final location will be. Hell is depicted by fire below the earth's surface, and heaven, above the clouds. Given the fact that the air is thin up there and non-existent in space and gravity issues abound, would you be better off heading off to hell with some marshmallows to toast? It may explain why bodies are burnt or buried in the ground. Launched up to heaven, people may come down with a thud.

Because the after-life is not known, people may make their own judgements about it and how they should spend their lives. Some will try to do anything and everything they can while they are alive. Others will live a staider life hoping that there is an after-life and thus go to the front of the queue for heaven. Most however will have a foot in both camps and many of these will not even begin to wonder and question until their final breaths are being taken. Then the regrets will come into play. Atheists and believers generally have no regrets. Agnostics may have many either way. Perhaps God, if there is one, should intervene and give some certainty.

Religion, God, faith, heaven and hell are just words. There import however is very strong. For some they are the reason for existence. For others they have no significance at all. To me, however each has a question mark after them. They make me wonder about life and wondering about life just makes it all the more interesting, confusing too granted, but interesting nevertheless.

Perhaps an area worth exploring is the concept of the egg with the albumen being the support structure, i.e. the world around us, and the yolk being life itself. Were they created separately, the albumen first obviously, or were they created in unison? If so, is mankind destroying that unison. One could also ask which came first the creator or the egg? It is the same with any theory including the big bang. What came before the big bang and what caused it? In a religion how many children asked the simplest yet most complex question of all, "Who made God?" I am not disparaging religion, scientists or even chickens by asking the child-like question. In essence the how is not important, nor is the who. It is the why that many people shy away from because it is the hardest to grapple with. Life including humankind evolved, but why? What was the purpose?

If indeed there is a purpose. Religions have imposed a purpose and for a lot of them it is a self-interest purpose because they gain power and control from it. What if we are all out of control and our yolk interacting with the albumen is all there is? Should we just enjoy it while we can?

Is life nothing more than a huge jigsaw puzzle and we are just pieces that somehow try to fit in? We link with others at times. Many find the perfect fit all around and never move far from that original position. Others find that, although they may link well with some around them, they are still out of place. Some are discarded and struggle to find their right place at all. But how many of us stop to look at what the big picture could be, what it entails and the minute detail needed to make it.

Is it better to wait until the picture becomes clearer so that you know where you fit in? If you do are you merely wasting time by not at least trying? And by waiting are you preventing those close by from being able to join? It seems that trial and error is an option but do you become discouraged when you keep failing to find where you fit in? There is no instruction manual and no simple logic in this most complex of all puzzles.

A strategy of grouping together pieces of similar shape, or colour could be seen to be advantageous, but it could also prove to be counterproductive if those are the wrong criteria or wrong assumptions are being made. Merely asserting that you are right doesn't make it so. The pieces look quite similar but there are almost microscopic differences which allow the individuality of each piece but also inhibit easy fits.

To build the whole picture is every piece necessary and of equal value? This is an edgeless puzzle and the pieces themselves only have a short life span before needing to be replaced. They will be replaced but not with an identical piece so no matter how malleable each appears to be, the replacement will not ever fill the same void.

There are an infinite number of pieces in the puzzle, each needing to interact with other pieces. The biggest difficulty that is faced however is that the picture is constantly changing and the interlocking links are tenuous. The puzzle rapidly and exponentially expands over time and the position of any given piece may need to change to adapt to the whole puzzle. How many of us can and are willing to do that without knowing what the big picture is and the importance of our role in it?

ARE WE CAPABLE OF REDEMPTION AND ATONEMENT?

The idea that one can seek redemption and atonement for mistakes merely by saying a few prayers seems somehow paltry if the action of a person has severely damaged or changed the lives of others. People will tell you to move on and that you can't change anything, but the sense of guilt cannot readily be assuaged with a few words. Just saying "sorry" doesn't cut it for many people. That guilt can live with them like a cancer for the rest of their lives. Having developed ethics and morals, some people who do something which compromises those, find it difficult to move forward and believe that there is a greater price to pay than mere words. For them no amount of money, time or action can ever right for them the terrible wrong that they believe they have done.

Others have thicker skins, and are less troubled by their conscience or are far more practical and can set the misdeed aside so as to not spoil the rest of their life. Spilt milk and no tears for them. Excuses can be made and justifications can be explained, but even these rankle the wrongdoer who thought he or she was so much more in control of the situation. When their world falls apart and impacts on the lives of others, they realise they were not in control of things around them and indeed even themselves. Is that what upsets them more than the effect they had on others? Perhaps it is a complex combination of the two. Deep undying regret grows malignantly inside them because they find out that they weren't the sort of person they perceived themselves to be, and/or they see and have, daily reminders of what their actions have done.

Can you be indemnified against your own sins? Who would underwrite such an insurance policy? Religions seem to have ways and means of doing it, allowing sinners to wipe the slate clean. Courts can too, using diminished capacity clauses or by setting community acceptable punishments. What if one's morals and ethics prohibit the use of the "Get out of Gaol free" card; where do you stand? The millstone that you have placed around your neck may not be obvious to those around you, but the weight seems to grow over time and the excuses and rationalisation that you had earlier on, don't seem to hold much water anymore. Will atonement ever come to your own satisfaction or will it still be there until the day you die and you carry it with you to your grave? Post mortem autopsies probably aren't sophisticated enough yet to analyse the guilt.

Forgiveness can come from those whom have been affected, but that may not be enough for the people who cannot forgive themselves. Where do these people go to from there? Who do they turn to? Religion will offer succour and sanctuary. Psychological counselling can also assist; but when these aren't enough, how do those people live with themselves? Is it a case of merely just putting one foot in front of the other and plodding on until the mental anguish eases or death removes all pain? Do they have to deal with the roller coaster ride of life knowing that there will be more and steeper downs than ups?

No doctor can excise the malignant cancer of guilt for some people. You can't change the cause, merely treat the symptoms in a palliative care manner. Those who believe in an afterlife or reincarnation, hope for a new start and to take on the learnings from their current life. Those who don't believe, endure rather than enjoy life; for no matter what they try to do to lessen that guilt and provide atonement to the people they have affected, they still carry that burden with them.

Wiping the slate clean after doing the time for the crime, is not available to some. For them it is not as easy as all that. The conscience of a person is a mysterious thing. Some say it is where the brain and the soul are connected. No-one has a clear conscience on everything that they have done, even if they try to rationalise everything. So, the pathway between the brain and soul is blocked to a certain extent. How big the occlusion is allowed to become depends on the morals and ethics one lives by. For those that aspire to higher ones of each, the damage caused by a fall from grace severely restricts that arterial path.

What constitutes a sin or mistake is different for everybody and the severity of that sin is likewise different, based on people's different morals and ethics. Therein lies the conundrum for any religious organisation which determines what the punishment and or atonement must be. The redemption required must be around what the wrongdoer believes to be fair. Too lenient or too harsh and the wrongdoer may seriously question the moral stance the religion is applying. In a confessional situation the redemption is kept between the priest and the sinner and thus there is no way for others to gauge, even if they know what the sin is, just what level of atonement must be made. In law however, the wrongdoer has some idea of the consequence. But what if the sin is seen as severe by the perpetrator but not even regarded as such by either the law or the religion? The sinner can only punish him or herself for crossing that moral or ethical line that the individual has in place. That level of redemption may be more than what is required for far more heinous crimes, in that it is long lasting, ever present in the form of guilt and reduces the person's feeling of self-worth quite severely. What is fair and just for one person may be totally different for another, because the consciences of individuals differ greatly between people.

So, where does one develop a conscience? The issue arises very early on in life as children learn what is right and wrong according to their parents or guardians. It is gradually refined through learning, observing and experience until a sense of values becomes more rigidly defined and absorbed into the psyche of a person. Religions do have a large say in developing these ethical and moral values for many people. Whether that is a good or bad thing is dependent on your views on religion. As we grow older, those rigid rules get massaged and altered gradually as we test them in different circumstances but a core set of beliefs remain. Everyone's set of beliefs is slightly different and that helps the individuality of a person come to the fore. Relationships can be built on these core beliefs and can also be destroyed by them. Transgressions that go against a partner's beliefs can dissolve a relationship and that is quite commonplace. Transgressions by yourself against your own core beliefs can be far more devastating. Disappointing someone else can weigh heavily on you. Disappointing yourself can crush you completely.

How many of us would love to go back in some time machine and make changes to the decisions that we made in the past? However, to paraphrase Doc' Emmett Brown from "Back to the Future", that would destroy the time/space equilibrium. Many people live their lives with a what if mentality that they can't shake. They can identify the turning point, even allocate the reasoning why but they can't alter that decision. Tormented by that frustration they seek forgiveness from those whose lives they have affected, but even if that is received, they can't forgive themselves. The shame and blame are things that endure and no amount of consoling and counselling will appease these people's consciences. How many of these people would be grateful if they could live with a lie, bury the past or "suck it up princess"?

What many do is sacrifice happiness in the process. Whenever chances for happiness arrive, they are shrouded in the darkness of previous guilt and thus not seen or the opportunities not taken up. The conduit between the brain and soul, the conscience, becomes further blocked. If happiness should occur, then guilt arises from even daring to be happy once again. The glass is half empty all the time and continually being drained without the chance of being replenished. By seeing the negative all the time, there is a high degree of chance that depression or reliance on legal and illegal drugs will occur. These will just exponentially increase the downward spiral.

Were these people destined to follow this labyrinth of passageways into the depths of despair? Was it because they set themselves too high a standard of morals and ethics and fail to take into account the human factor? Was the pushing of that high standard by their parents, religion and society around them setting them up for a fall? Were they just victims of circumstances beyond their control and just happened to be in a certain place at a certain time? They have been walking a high wire for much of their life with no safety net except perhaps friends, family or religious beliefs to potentially soften their landing.

The trouble is that no-one really knows why. To hear that it is all part of God's masterplan would make someone think that the masterplan sucked and that God was an uncaring being. Why would a kind and benevolent god put an individual through such mental torture? If it was social upbringing, why would family, friends and the broader community allow the formation of such high standards in an individual without explaining that people are allowed to and are prone to making mistakes? If it is a genetic disposition, what can be done to breed out this debilitating factor?

Judgement is being passed on an individual by that individual without some knowledge and reference point except what sense of values they have acquired. Often it is done in secret as is the self-inflicted punishment. Families, friends and communities in these modern times are far more detached than in previous centuries. They may not become aware of the problem until it is too late and the individual has decided that any sort of atonement is not good enough and so life is not worth living. Suicide is such a taboo subject that people don't know how to raise it if they think someone is in trouble. No training is given to those in the position to administer first aid. Someone whose core beliefs have been severely trampled needs very little to push them over the edge, so delicacy is needed. Those closest to that person may not be able to emotionally remove themselves enough to apply that first aid and so a new form of guilt is passed on.

People's core values and beliefs are rarely enunciated aloud. To say, "This is what I believe" is a rarity these days as people lack confidence and tend to fit in with "the norm". Public image has become very much more important too. There seems to be a much higher value being placed on being accepted by others than accepting yourself. Consequently, the sense of values gets repressed and this makes an unexpected clash with them far more severe. There is a lot of money invested in educating children how to read, write, be numerate and have good computer literacy. However, the most valuable asset to the community, the individual, needs also to be taught how to live with their own individuality, their beliefs, morals and ethics. They need to learn how these are developed and how they can best be managed. Society doesn't need clones but does need thinking creative people who can live with who they are, know that they will make mistakes and know how to deal with atoning for those mistakes and live with them.

WHY IS EVERYONE DIFFERENT?

Everyone has their own reality. From the most ostentatious to the poorest humblest person on the planet, each has their own reality and no two are the same. It is those variations that make the rich tapestry of human existence that has seen our world progress and indeed regress since time began. It is how we have been able to somehow marry everyone's reality into a workable society that is the most amazing aspect of the growth of humanity. But sadly, that is in itself the weakness that has the capacity to destroy all that has gone before.

To make any society function at its best there needs to be an acceptance of others' reality. The initial problem that most people face is that they can't understand why people do what they do and why their own moral compass seems to be pointing in a different direction. It is impossible to live in another person's shoes 24 hours a day for a lifetime and so no real understanding of what makes another person tick can occur. It is dangerous and dismissive to make assumptions based on limited knowledge and because each individual has a complex pattern of behaviours and reasons for those behaviours, it is nigh on impossible to gather enough information to make a rational judgement. When you throw in the issue of the subjectivity of the person making the judgement the difficulty grows exponentially. It is better to assess a person, if indeed you must assess someone, based on their impact, both good and bad, on others.

To allow us to comprehend and organise the vast scope of people out there we have adapted over time the ability to stereotype groups of people we encounter. Our brain is not properly equipped to manage the numbers and so we sift them in a mail type sorting house. This means that there are very basic structures of sorting and individual peccadillos and idiosyncrasies are easily swept aside or dismissed to accommodate the process. In effect we are culling individual identities, their truths and realities. Ethnicity, culture, intelligence, sexual persuasion and even physical appearances are the most normally used identifiers and sadly we sort according to the lowest common denominators. A perfect example is where someone says they have some good friends who are devout worshippers at a mosque and are lovely people, "but you certainly can't trust those Muslims". The irony is lost on many people. Because we do not have the time, patience and interest in a lot of cases, to look beyond the initial identifying factors, we miss so much. We shut out whole groups of people out of our lives because they are different according to our mindset, whereas in reality they aren't very different at all.

Man is a primitive species as we don't have the capacity to think beyond ourselves, to rationalise our role in the greater scheme of things both here on planet earth and in the wider universe. Because we see ourselves as the vastly superior entity here with the highest functioning brain, we assume that we are the same in the universe. This is a construct man lives by and inculcates in future generations. We may have a higher functioning brain and can harness much of what the world offers does that make us necessarily superior? We currently are destroying our own planet in a way that no other creature could or would. How smart is that? We cause the destruction of our own kind through wars based on in many cases greed and stupidity. Again, not conclusive proof of our superior intellect. We kill for the fun and sake of killing. Like so many things humankind does, we do it because we can. Other species do things to survive and we see a natural beauty and harmony in that, but we choose not to follow. Ironic isn't it.

By grouping people in our minds, we show how primitive we are and how little we have moved on since we first arrived as a species. Our world is organised into nations and territorial states that are defended at enormous cost. Might is right and it is okay to exploit those who have less. Great mantra. We could feed all the starving and house all the homeless by spending money on them rather than on defence. Even in our cities and towns we discriminate according to lowest common factors. The partitions are very real as separate areas and indeed ghettoes of races, colours and creeds. It seems to comfort our brains so much to have things sorted like with like. The notion has been around so long that it has become normalised and people feel secure being with others of the same "kind" and knowing "their place". It has been rationalised into our education system too.

Education used to be the key for advancement but we now see that there are strings, often financial strings, attached and the haves are trained higher so they can keep having. It has become a self-fulfilling prophecy, rather than a chance for social mobility. Curriculum is different between groups; standards are not comparable but more importantly opportunities are very much unequal. The other aspect that becomes apparent is that differences are reinforced through the curriculum itself in many countries. Some is subtle in some countries but much of it is blatant. Roles for gender, attitudes towards different religions and economic status etc. are woven through literature and the contesting of ideas regarding variation of these mores is limited at best.

Most people are too busy eking out an existence to stop and reflect on things beyond their most immediate and basic needs. It becomes much easier for others to suborn these people and subjugate them. That is why they become easy prey to mass media campaigns of advertising and indoctrination. If a "lie" is told often enough it soon becomes accepted as a "truth". Any individual, any nation who wishes to vanquish a large group will target the intelligent people in a society first as they are the ones who often can become the dissidents, marshal support and are less likely to believe in the propaganda that is being fed to them. The subtleties of capitalism and the establishment of a belief system that everyone can be rich, famous, have a "perfect body" is a perfect example of a subliminal attack on the intelligent members of society. Many fall for the notion and can't see beyond the name brands and must have items that have no more intrinsic value than their much cheaper counterparts. It is nowhere near as blatant but nevertheless very destructive. It encourages people to assess another person's value based on their wealth in monetary terms and not on their value to society. One wonders whether the poorer people at times are filled with envy and a little hope; and their wealthier neighbours even consider other people's realities and backstories. Societies and religions have to keep the balance and blend of hope, possibility of change in circumstances, and the actual reality just right or a threshold is crossed where chaos and disbelief can destroy everything.

The imposition of a class system has always had a deleterious effect on society. The justification for the imposition is that helps establish an order and structure. However, whilst it gives a means of people knowing they have a role, it very often decides that role and leaves no avenue to escape from that role. It is the ultimate stereotyping. It encourages those who are in a higher stratum to consider others below of little or no importance and that these people have no thoughts, emotions, needs, wants that should be discussed or taken into account. In colonial days, civilisations were destroyed that were vastly superior than those of the invaders and individuals were used as cannon fodder to achieve what?

Over time humans have created the artificial construct of religion to help make sense of it all. The mere fact that we have such a small time on earth and no knowledge of what happens afterwards, added to our reasoning mind has encouraged philosophers, cultures and individuals to develop morals and ethics that try to ascribe some purpose to and understanding of why we are on the planet in the first place. From the earliest times religions have developed through a range of different cultures. They have served several functions including instilling social rules, passing on folklore and uniting groups. Often, they have developed around people of note who speak many of their own truths that others can associate with. This voicing of what some people as populist homilies is an important element in any society. They become the joint truths of a group and unite that group even stronger. If they tie in with previous understandings of a group, then these religions develop and grow and become part of the folklore, the morals and social structure.

There are many issues that have clouded religions for centuries. The first is the strange way that myths and legends have tried to be incorporated along with parts of other religions to provide an all-encompassing product that a number of people would accept. This has led to a cornucopia of strange and often contradictory maxims that are open to interpretation.

Secondly, are the attempts to put the origin of life, beginnings of mankind and the afterlife into a tight binding explanation that would have been better to have been stated as "we don't know" as further learning and scientific discovery have debunked most of the known theories in religions already.

Thirdly, we have the rise of a priest class who have self-proclaimed powers to administer rites, determine rules and structures of the religion and "tax" believers by means of tithes and donations. As well-meaning as these priests may be, they have also been shown to have political and secular desires beyond what they espouse.

Fourthly, is the belief that only their religion is correct and their version of that religion in fact is correct and must be inculcated into the minds of non-believers. Those who will not conform are to be castigated, excommunicated, exiled or even killed. The mindset that when the ideology and religion are united and indoctrinated in a social group as the one real truth, all will be well, is a fallacy. Because everyone is coming from a different starting point, has different life experiences and thought processes, there can be no one real truth but a plethora of near truths that are as diverse as the people who exist.

It is the teachings and their interpretation by priests, the application of rules, the indoctrination, the non-acceptance of others and the discrimination that plagues religions. These things cause a rise in the numbers of non-believers and a move away from one of the strongest pillars of our society in the past. As our society has become more educated and materialistic, the strength of religious bodies has weakened. This has caused the really valuable parts of religion such as awareness and acceptance of others, common understandings of how societies function well, and basic tenets of rights and obligations to be lost or at best diluted.

Over the years there have been attempts to hijack that religious construct to discriminate and to dismiss the value of another person's reality. Zealots and factionalists of a religion have tried to use their own religions to create a new and stronger religion that tries to divide and then conquer their own religion and then take on the other religions. Part of the issue for the rise of these groups has been the economic divisions that interpreters of laws have encouraged and maintained. Wars for centuries have been cloaked with religious reasons as some sort of justification for the real core motive. While most religions espouse the need to help their fellow man, wars are based on greed and depriving one group of people for the benefit of other people. Economics, not religious beliefs, fuel wars. Religion is merely the excuse, but it does allow those with less awareness to be lulled into joining up. From the crusades to the latest jihads it has been about one group trying to dominate another. It is powered by greed and envy and sugar-coated with a veneer of religious fervour. Stripped down to the basic tenets of their faith, most religions would not countenance war at all. It all comes back to the layers of interpretation and spin that have been put on those simple social rules that underpin all religions. Parables and fables, myths and legends are added to explain the meaning of all religions. Yet these are now taken as truths and justification for the subjugation of others and ultimately to the hijacking of religions, rise in cults and indeed justification for war.

The use of religious interpretations has become more prevalent as the main structure of each has fractured and those fractures in turn fracture, inevitably pitting like against like and against those different as well. Stereotyping according to religious beliefs doesn't take into account different factions and cults and indeed the beliefs and realities of individuals. To be tarred with the one brush can force people to rebel and unite and be thus be counterproductive to attempts to create harmony. All followers of Islam are not the same but are treated the same by many westerners. In Northern Ireland neighbours were forced to become enemies because of the type of Christianity the followed. What is lost in such schisms, is that people are people first. They merely want their basic needs met and will align with those that can supply those basic needs first. However, leaders exploit the situation often associated with these living conditions and link it with religious ideals of factions to create far more powerful and larger groups of people.

Since primitive times the enforcement of ideologies to develop cohesion including codes of behaviour, rules or laws by leaders have been put in place. In order to make the whole thing work, common understandings are set out and ongoing education to support and indoctrinate those understandings has been essential to maintain the structure of a society. There is validity in such methods as that binds groups together in harmony and can protect them from outside influences. It is a double-edged sword as the same education can turn out merely clones of others and squash any other thinking may mean a group of people will not progress because different thinking is not permitted. Various isms over time have used both religious and political education to control and manipulate large groups of people. Anyone querying curriculum content has been labelled anything from a heretic, mentally disturbed to being an insurgent.

Separation of church, state and education must not only be on the surface but also underpin the structure of society. To many, that would seem a recipe for disruption, but the alternative is a greater issue where over-control can lead to revolution and anarchy. An open and free society allows divergence, questioning, and voicing of concerns. However, an open and free society can only function well if freedoms are allied to an awareness of every individual's rights, an understanding that choices come with responsibilities, and that opportunities must be fair and equitably distributed. Originally these have come from common understandings about right and wrong and now are enshrined in common law and bills of rights. Proscribed and limited education runs contrary to the rights of individuals.

Reality is a nominal issue at best. Few people consider their own reality because they are too busy living. Even fewer consider that other people's realities are different and just as important. However, it is inescapable that all these realities affect the way we live, the precepts we hold and ultimately the meaning we get out of our life as short as it is. One of the best things that we can do is to give people time, space and guidance to think about their own existence. We need to encourage them to recognise that other people have an existence too that is equally important. We also should recognise that, as we live in an interconnected society, one person's reality affects everyone else's. It is time for the world to have a reality check.

WHAT GOES ON IN OUR HEADS?

"Space – the final frontier" This oft used Star Trek quote doesn't define what space it refers to – inner or outer space. We have spent billions of dollars probing outer space for a few humans to walk on the moon and for a few scientists to play with a few robot satellites and remote-control toys on planets, yet by far the biggest challenge lies in the space between our ears.

There is enough intelligence and intellectual know-how to solve all the world's ills already but it is not being directed towards objectives that will make our planet sustainable, socially and environmentally. What drives greed? What drives aggression? We have inbuilt psychological mechanisms that divide humanity into "haves" and "have-nots" and "want somes" and "enough is never enoughs".

We cloak them in civility with Geneva conventions and religious and ethical dictums but these just mask the fact that although we have come a long way in terms of scientific knowledge and application, we have progressed little since our evolution from wild animal and caveman; except that we have become more sophisticated in the way that we kill and humiliate others.

The so called seven deadly sins of: wrath, greed, sloth, pride, lust, envy and gluttony are actually what drives humanity, but also will drive humanity to its doom as they are taken to excess by individuals, companies and nations alike. Might is right is the law of the jungle and as much as we can and do intellectualise any argument to explain and condone an action, it all comes back to the same law. If we can find the "I can so I will" gene and put in place a self-control mechanism we may have a chance.

Many people argue that it is man's emotions that make us different and set us above the rest of the animal world. But are we in fact above? We look down on animals and often Disneyfy them with human characteristics, but in many instances their ability to work in harmony with each other as a family unit, a pack, a herd, a species and a group of different species shows us that we have a long way to go to reach that level of sophistication. For whales each member of a pod is as important as each other with the exception that the young are more important as they are the future. They will gather around and support one another in a way that humans don't do perhaps as readily in this modern world. The social animals like bees and ants rely on each other and there appears no "me-me-meness" in their everyday life. Their evolution as a society is on a slow upward progression; yet humans want to evolve right here and right now.

If you look at the herding animals in Africa, they migrate in search of food. Many species inter-relate to work together for the common good of the whole herd. In humans, next door neighbours and even nations can't do that. Because of our so-called sophistication, our desire to have everything now, we are losing the ability to work together for the common good. Our government systems are adversarial and groups within in them won't and don't work together. For wanting immediate change, we are locked in by barriers that slow us down. Animals don't build fences. They may mark territory but that is a survival mechanism based on food supply rather than on avarice. Rarely will they kill their own species, yet humans do so on a very regular basis, in some cases with delight and no compassion. In a perverse sort of way, we will cry over a sick puppy but show no remorse about the deaths of humans overseas that we have labelled as refugees, insurgents or inconsequential.

It is that labelling that is one of the more galling aspects of the human condition. We stereotype individuals; which for all the pride we take as a sophisticated reasoning society, displays just how ignorant and uninformed we are. It can be argued that it is our brains way of dealing with large numbers, yet we apply the process indiscriminately and discriminate against others. If someone looks different, speaks differently, has a different religious cultural or economic background, they are to be feared or envied but rarely to be accepted. Do we actually believe they might think about things the way we do?

That is a major question that needs to be asked. "Why do we think the way we do?" Is it environmental or physical in its origin? Or perhaps a combination of both – the old nature versus nurture argument. If we waste time however on arguing that point, we will get nowhere and have put up yet another barrier, another fence that smarter species would simply avoid or walk around. Some will argue that we need to know whether think is brought about by genetic predisposition or social factors so that we have a starting point and that without that knowledge we will only treat the symptoms and not the source. However, treating the symptoms may give us time to find a cure. And a cure is what we need or humanity will implode.

The symptoms are quite obvious. Individuals want more and are becoming increasingly less worried about how they achieve that. There is a loose fabric of laws that may hold some back for a short time and also keep lawyers employed on finding ways around them. Some of the rules are based on ethics from religious ideals. Some of the rules are made by those who rule and designed to keep the rulers in their place and their subjects in their place. In a market place environment we are encouraged to believe everyone is equal and yet also want more and more and so improve on what we have to keep up with those who are ahead of us but who are still our equals. However, this means that the rich get richer and the poor can't get enough. Eventually the poor will rise up and the social cohesiveness of the fabric of society is torn apart. Humans seem to learn nothing from history.

One solution is to examine the reason for greed and when enough is enough. One question the wealthy have in front of them every day is the price they pay for security, anonymity if it is sought, privacy and exclusion from everyday social life. This applies not only to individuals but families and nations. Many nations spend billions of dollars on defence to retain what they have but in doing so create an armaments and defence industry that needs constant supply of conflicts to stay viable. Like the use of electricity in the late 1800's which spawned a host of electric powered inventions so that more electricity could be used, the defence industry will fight hard to ensure somewhere in the world, war is happening. If the money spent on defence was spent on feeding the poor, ensuring health and prosperity then there would be no need for a defence industry. How as a logical reasoning society can we continue to let war happen? We receive subliminal messages daily that there is a better life to be had but that someone also wants to take away what we have already got. If we could flag and convert these messages and run them through a psychological bullshit detector then the world would be a much better place. If we revered the elderly and protected and educated the young as more so-called primitive cultures and creatures do, then some of that greed and envy culture might eventually fade. To turn off the greed in humans would be a major medical and social breakthrough.

If you sit as a casual observer on a group of "everyday" people in almost every culture, you would notice that despite the language and other superficial differences many things are common with others; in particular their needs.

Basic needs including food, water, clothing, shelter and health have a higher priority for those who are poor and each day for them so much time, thought and energy is expended on trying to get just these needs met. If they aren't met, they revert to the flight or fight mode of operation. This explains uprisings and refugees. If the needs aren't met, they become triggers for war, famine and disease, all of which are preventable. It is essential using basic logic that the wealthy should intervene or they may become targeted. However, the intervention is far more effective if it is in the form of support rather than attack. Foreign aid has a more long-lasting effect than a military incursion. But an arms driven, wealth creating capitalistic society often baulks at giving food and medicine away for free. Bombs create opportunities for rebuilding physical structures and further wealth creation. Free medicine and food can help rebuild societies themselves and make them stronger for the next time a needs crisis occurs. The world already has enough food to feed those on the planet and enough weapons to destroy it as well. Sadly, because the human condition is gravitating towards a less caring and sharing mode of thinking we are heading towards a self-destruction phase. If we could do some more research into how we can put compassion and the humanity back into humans, we may stand a chance of survival.

Some of the next level of needs to be met include: education, social interaction, sense of self-worth and sense of belonging. For many people that means living in a community and constructing something, be it physical, educational, social or emotional, that is of benefit to that community. Providing employment and thus the means to earn money to purchase basic necessities has long been seen as the catalyst for maintaining the status quo in a community. Harnessing the skills of an individual or a group of people makes them more productive and delivers better outcomes for a community. That is one reasons people are put in prisons. Punishment is meted out in the form of deprivation of this second set of needs. One wonders how asylum seekers feel incarcerated in facilities that barely meet first level needs and being deprived of almost all second level needs. They have left war torn countries merely to survive and yet they are in an almost worse situation.

Societies promote the myth that if you work hard you can have everything. It is a myth because the type of work and quality of work has already been socially levelled often by the wealthy. Productivity gains are what are being sought in areas where productivity can't be measured accurately. Education, health and community services are such areas. But we buy the myth because if we don't, we may become ostracised from the community that we wish to belong to. Churches, schools, governments and the media foster the myth, often knowing full well that it is snake oil that they are selling. Managing this level of needs takes all forms and can be very restrictive in totalitarian regimes or quasi democratic ones too. However, it is very effective in managing first world problems. Telling people what they need to know, what they can and cannot say or do whilst at the same time as massaging their egos, offering socially interesting activities; is a classic method of control. Perhaps money could be spent investigating why humans have the urge to control others.

While we are mapping the human brain and working out what does what perhaps some of the other deadly sins could have their key activators found and hopefully able to be isolated and manipulated. I am not talking about a Brave New World scheme of chemical therapy but informing people what their triggers are and what they can do to gain mastery over these. We are bombarded with sexual situations via a burgeoning media which knows that sex sells. People are continually told that the sex they are having could be a whole lot better. Different forms of voyeuristic sexual activity and pornography are more readily available and the moral and ethics of a past social construct are forever being challenged. For the greater part of the information available and provided it is a marketing tool but it merely reinforces for many people that one's own gratification is the reason for existence. Consequently, the information being provided to children is often distorted, misguided and confusing. Extremist groups argue for sexual freedom or for sexual restraint in all aspects. It is unhealthy to promote lust as a virtue and just as unhealthy to cast it as something evil. It is a function of human nature and a person's self-management of it is part of their development as they grow. Laws have been set up to protect the young, the vulnerable and those who are forced into sexual activity. These laws have come from within a society that saw that protection was needed and also some freedom from repression was also necessary. Like most laws they differ between cultures, nations and even within communities and continue to be modified as a society develops.

There is a proclivity for anger to be seen as being healthy if it is let out. However, the tendency for a human to express this in a way that doesn't impinge on others isn't easily translated in to safe practice. Given their growing inability to care about the feelings of others, humans are developing ambivalence to violence and its effects. Once again laws have been put in place but the desire for understanding for actions often gets in the way of a clear understanding of what a victim goes through. Too often leniency is given because the cause has so many mitigating circumstances and the initiator of the violence can be seen as a victim rather than the victim him/herself. A slap on the wrist doesn't cause all violent perpetrators of crime to desist. Rather it encourages them to understand that the effects of the crime don't count for much and reinforces that victims don't count for much either. What societies should do is look for a middle ground and work on crime prevention rather than deal with the after effects. People with anger issues often reach a point of no return when the fuse is lit. If we knew more about how the brain functions then perhaps anger management by an individual may be able to become effective. Issues such as domestic violence, riots and mob violence which account for many crimes would benefit from proper research. Anger issues are often seen early on in a child's development but can also occur later on in individuals by some trauma or by not having basic and secondary needs met. Often it is the response to something that is perceived as being unfair and perhaps that unfairness is not explained to the individual or ways of addressing or accepting that unfairness. With people being so consumed with themselves they become oblivious of others around them who may be treated unfairly. When those people respond with anger, the response is usually negative and can exacerbate the situation. Once again, the symptom or outcome is being dealt with not the underlying cause. Parents and education institutions are struggling to bring into being a sense of values and ethics for the young in particular. The breakdown of social networks in communities is a major concern as the delivering of a moral and ethical framework used to be the responsibility of a tribe, extended family or village. Nowadays tribal structures have disappeared. Extended families are literally kilometres away and villages are now huge urban complexes where neighbours and connecting social structures are more isolated than they ever were. Humans are now living a lot closer to each other but have never been more apart.

The issue of laziness or sloth is often raised to impugn the reputation of those who are unemployed or who have the choice of working for barely more than a pittance or waiting until work is available where the pay is a bit more than a subsistence level. Judging others based on one's own perceptions has always been a human failing and preoccupation. It also helps to keep people in their place. The reasons for sloth are many and varied, ranging from medical, psychological to being over indulged. Instead of berating someone whom you consider is not contributing to the community, perhaps investigating why, providing opportunities and supporting them would be more fruitful. Animals that live in groups do that, but humans have "outgrown" that. As we become more civilised, we have become less civil. We choose to castigate and condemn as a first course of action rather than lend a hand. If we help others to feel worthwhile their independence will be fostered. Charity is not just giving a handout, but recognising a need and offering hope and helping to build resilience. I am sure that in the deep recesses of the cerebellum where it has been pushed in our modern world thinking, there is a charitable element that can be made to be more readily accessed.

When you ask people why they work so hard often the response is that they wish to earn enough to find time to sit back and do nothing. Indeed, that is what some of the richest people in the world do in comparison to those who aren't having their basic needs met as these people have no choice. A whole industry has been derived to meet the needs of those who wish to do as little as possible. To ensure that is a viable industry low wages are paid to its workers and that also precludes these people from mixing with those that they serve. This service industry was once catered for by slavery. People would capture and trade other humans so that they could do the work that they didn't want to do. They would then beat these slaves for not working hard enough, when they themselves did very little. For one person it was sloth, for another it was leisure. Low wages and keeping people in penury is seen as making these people feel worthwhile yet it is only a little better than slavery. It continues the divide between rich and poor and it actually encourages people to do nothing as the thought of striving hard for advancement when no advancement is possible gains traction. It is not an attitude but a response to the unspoken feedback that people get.

A work ethic is developed over time and so is an unemployed ethic. If children see their parents forced to live off welfare because no work is available then that is the ethic they will grow up with. A hard-working parent who gets little joy out of working and out of life can unwittingly encourage children not to develop a work ethic. Parents who do everything for their children can also unwittingly curb a work ethic as the children believe that someone will give them everything on a plate. Getting the balance right is extremely difficult. A work ethic will differ between individuals, families and cultures. A community needs people to work but people need to enjoy life at the same time. Investigating how the brain handles those two contrasting needs and all the competing outside influences could help humans construct a worthwhile living and working environment.

Since when has it been wrong to admit a mistake? It used to be a sign of growing maturity. With our politicians never owning up to a mistake, surely we must question their maturity. One of society's modern-day issues is that the ownership of a mistake is fraught with danger. There is an associated possibility of litigation and ongoing public humiliation. The media is forever chasing "got ya" moments as they titillate their readers/viewers. Being famous, a celebrity or a tall poppy opens you up to being cut down and ridiculed over seemingly trivial matters. People now go around in fear of open communication lest they be treated derisively in the modern-day culture of put downs. Someone is accused by a tabloid newspaper and it is front page news. If they have been wrongly accused the apology or retraction is buried inside weeks later. Headlines are often distorted to capture attention. Photos may also not match the content but any attempt to hold the tabloid to account is labelled as an attempt to stop the freedom of the press.

For many people they pride themselves on their reputations and the ongoing fear of failure and ridicule can stifle experimentation, invention and creativity and the community as well as the individual suffers. It seems that to build yourself up to stand out from the rest these days is by not being better but belittling those around you. Pride and envy are two fascinating traits of humanity to study. They can drive people to excel but also stop people from achieving. The dichotomy is very apparent in the scientific community where pride exists as a driver for new achievements but can hold back any shared work as credit for those achievements is not readily shared. If the benefit is for the community does it matter who brought about that benefit? Apparently, it does as schools, universities and research institutions which run on a shoe string budget can only gain more grants through recognition. Our society rewards success and abhors failure yet strangely failures are what lead to successes. Do pharmaceutical companies willingly share their research findings and make medicines cheap for the underprivileged? Certainly not; they are seeking to cover research costs and make handsome profits. They take pride in their stock market price and want to be the envy of others.

Humans now take pride in their material possessions and their wealth. Many take pride in their personal accomplishments and some also in their pedigree which gives them satisfaction that they have continued on the family tradition usually based on wealth of an antecedent. For different cultures that lineage has spiritual and traditional values. For some that means doing the same job as their forebears, taking over a family business, having a family member become a member of the priesthood. This has enabled a caste or class system to develop and strict provisions insist that changing class is not done. Democracies also have an inbuilt class system based often on wealth and not necessarily on merit. Opportunities are denied to those who could advance themselves because they have been brought up on the wrong side of the tracks or whose parents aren't married. It is subtle in some instances as education is the main route to advancement and the notion of a private school and the old school tie excludes so many who will have their education stunted in poorly financed schools. A class system feeds on envy and pride. Those at the bottom envy those above. Those in the middle take pride in the fact that they are not at the bottom and envy those above. Those in the upper class are fully aware and take pride in the knowledge that others envy them.

Pride and envy are not sins, they are conditions forged by the structure of the society of humans. They are reinforced by everyday living conditions, the media, education and the control of wealth. How the mind deals with these outside pressures is worthy of study so that individuals can learn how to manage their own feelings and perhaps as a society change the social structure so that envy and pride have less of an effect.

The seven deadly sins are managed on a daily basis by individuals within a society because of laws, entrenched social structures and a code of ethics. If they weren't managed chaos and anarchy would ensue. However, between our ears is a massive force that enables us to assimilate all sorts of information into not only a survival mode of operation but a socially inclusive way of life. Greater research into this inner space could lead us into being better managers. Perhaps in the future people will:

take pride in their humility;

become gluttons for selflessness;

lust for opportunities to help others,

use sloth as a means of recharging their own batteries and smelling the roses,

envy those who have more time to support others

express anger in a positive way against those who discriminate, or physically or emotionally hurt others' and

be greedy for more knowledge and a better way of living for everyone.

One can only hope.

WHY ARE WOMEN SO COMMON IN HUMAN CARE FIELDS?

There is no doubt that the current social construct that we currently live in is almost arse about of what it should be. We reward and recognise the selfish; and the selfless get the leftovers. The people who serve the community in making it function as best as it can are often financially downtrodden and treated almost subserviently. Nurses, teachers, child care workers are just some who fail into that category. Whether through tradition, lack of other opportunities or maybe even because there is a desire to fulfil a caring role, women form the vast majority of the people in these careers.

Many women thus are always left behind financially. Many love their jobs, but their jobs don't reciprocate in terms of salary or social standing. Paying people according to their actual contribution to society would dramatically change that. A sporting star, a singer or a film actor may argue that they provide much more to more people than a nurse who cares for a dozen patients at a time, or a teacher who is in front of a class of twenty-five children. Perhaps comparisons such as these are useless, but they are built in and front and centre already to our society through recognition and financial gain.

Equal pay for equal work gets terribly confused when comparisons are made between different professions, especially when each professional body will not give an inch. Such protectionism extends even further because for some bodies they see no benefit in equalling the opportunities for those from low socio-economic backgrounds, different cultures and different genders. It is masked well to protect themselves from laws that frown on such things, but it is definitely there. Tokenism exists and one or two people who may be female, from a different culture and from a poor background are trotted out to show that you don't have to be rich white and male to fit in. However, if that is true, why are there so few who break the mould? Unfortunately, there won't be a big turnaround or even a discussion on the matter, for those ensconced at the top of the tree would be the ones who would benefit the least if changes in the status quo occurred.

Australia is not an egalitarian country as much as we try to pretend we are. We meekly follow past practices and imitate what others do overseas, even though those may not be best practices. We understand that education is the key to social mobility, wealth and lifestyle. Many people pay dearly for their children to go to elite private schools hoping that will ensure the next generation has greater success. However, many children's cards are already marked by their parents' own financial and social standing. So, many parents actually lose on the deal. You would think too that if education was such a vital tool, that those doing the face to face delivery of it would be paid well for their efforts. That doesn't happen because teachers have a poor social standing. The fact that they are mainly women, on the surface appears to diminish that value even more. There are unspoken social maxims built up over centuries that will take centuries to overturn.

There are more vocations open to women than ever before. Just how open they are is perhaps quite debatable. Fifty years ago, women were traditionally offered just a few choices: teaching, nursing, secretarial work, the garment trade or as shop assistants. These formed the bulk of the careers that women began, often only to forego when they became wives and/or mothers. Given the change in choices on offer, why are women still drawn in particular to teaching and nursing? Community expectations have increased of people in these careers as has public criticism. These careers pay poorly and often involve verbal, physical and emotional abuse, so what is the attraction?

Women have usually been depicted as the ones who are the caring nurturing types. Does the label match the genetic truth or have women been socialised to conform to this label? If the professions of teaching and nursing for example were rewarded as financially and had the same social status and recognition commensurate with architects and engineers, would more men be drawn to teaching and nursing? And would women opt for careers in engineering and architecture over teaching and nursing? In short, are women generally more suited to these latter ones. They have proven themselves over a long period of time to be better than many of their few male counterparts in teaching and nursing. It is the old nature versus nurture argument which will probably never be fully resolved. In the meantime, a restructure of the worth of professions would go a long way to alleviate the disadvantage that many community contributors, in particular women have facing them. Are teaching and nursing demeaned because they are areas women are in the majority? If so, what does that say about the way we treat and value women?

Questions to answer:

Do women feel obligated to go into careers of teaching and nursing?

Are they generally genetically programmed for caring roles?

Do women have the same opportunities extended to them in other occupations?

Are women still being channelled into caring roles?

Caring roles are seen as less valuable by society and offer lower wages. Why?

What would be a proper commensurate occupation to both teaching and nursing?

What impact/allowance is made for pregnancy and subsequent return to work in both teaching and nursing? Do similar things exist in more male dominated occupations?

When you are next in hospital, dropping a child off at childcare or at a school, ask yourself how much the person who will be looking after you or your child is actually worth; what they are contributing, not just to you or your child, but to the smooth running and future of our society.

WHY DO THINGS HAPPEN THE WAY THEY DO?

There are those who believe in a religion because the tenets of that gives them some meaning to their lives. There are others who do not and never question what the purpose for their own existence is. These may both be the lucky ones. Both are gainfully occupied in living a life that is laid out before them and they need not worry too much choosing the direction that they follow in life. A few continue to question the mystery of life itself, not trying to have imposed on it someone else's viewpoint on it, and disregard the possibility that there may not be any purpose at all. Some go blithely through from birth to death without even looking at the big picture. For many, just staying alive by getting the basic needs met is a struggle in itself and there is no time, energy and will to look beyond where their next meal is coming from. So much of our world which is rich in everything, yet it is inhabited by people living in poverty. Why?

Would other civilizations have lived in the past as we do today? Would other communities on other planets in the vast universe live the way we do? We have transcended our forebears in almost all facets of life, yet we have not come far. Some might say that we have actually gone backwards. The cultural and social divide between the haves and the have nots has widened and we accept that, are encouraged to accept that and our media, our educational institutions and our governments promote the idea that it is a good thing. But for whom? To aspire to greater things may be fine if those greater things are not just material things, but instead are kindness of heart, willingness to share, volunteering to help those less fortunate and all the finest of traits that past philosophers have put forward and that underpin most religions.

So why are we here in this time in this place? What has come before us? What will follow us? Just as any individual is not the centre of the universe and time did not commence at his or her birth, the Earth isn't either. When time on Earth ends for an individual, does anyone really notice? Does anyone validate that person's contribution to the whole universe? Given the vast number of beings that have lived and died since time began in this universe, does one being's life and death matter or make a difference. If not, why then bother having a life at all.

Existentialism is defined as a philosophy that emphasizes individual existence, freedom and choice. It is the view that
humans define their own meaning in life, and try to make rational decisions despite existing in an irrational universe.

It can be argued that people have many choices available to them throughout their lives that determine their destiny. This would give a lie to divine intervention at least in an everyday sense. However, the wealthier you are, the more educated you are and the safer you are, the vaster the number and range of choices. These people can also allow you to go back and try to remedy past mistakes. One significant other modifier in being able to determine your own destiny, is the cultural and social community that you are raised in and your place in it. In many societies, children have little or no say in important matters pertaining directly to them. In others, females can be added to the list. People are exposed to traditions and stereotypes and the freedom to be different is actively discouraged. Religions, schools, families and community standards can, and frequently often do, restrict any deviations and limit choices. So, there are caveats attached to the notion of existentialism.

Do they matter at all? How many times have people wanted a rewind or reset button to change their circumstances? How many people have enviously wished for a better life once they have seen others having it? Our media is full of envy, jealousy and greed disguised as being aspirational. And to what end? You come into the world with nothing and you leave it the same way. Few people acknowledge your entry and sometimes fewer, your exit.

Perhaps religions have it right by making life more predictable than the self-determination of existentialism. To not question why you are here is less time consuming, less stressful and offers more hope than trying to nut it all out and manage your own direction in life. Religions offer explanations for why things are the way they are. They also offer directions as to what course you should steer. A meaning of life, whether it is right or wrong, takes the pressure off and can allow you to just enjoy the living experience. Existentialists may waste valuable time, time better spent on exploring life, because they are just trying to make sense of it all. They rarely pause to accept the fact that they are in the here and now and that they should be grateful for that first and foremost. Their lives don't have to mean something or impact heavily on the whole universe to be significant. The significance can be just the opportunity to be alive even for a short amount of time.

History is a vast tableau across the universe. Even on earth it gets written and rewritten every day. What was important for one generation will not be for the next, although retro periods will occur frequently. Believing that you can shape the universe by what you achieve in the relatively short amount of time of a human life evokes a feeling of grandeur and omnipotence not deserved. Just as a wave washes away a footprint on a beach, a person's influence is quickly gone without a trace.

Your own individual will, will not change everything that comes your way. Factors outside of your control have already influenced you as you have grown up. These have partially predetermined your present and your future. It is almost impossible to completely set these aside as they have already shaped your attitudes and your beliefs. These attitudes and beliefs will continue to change as you interact with people and events around you. It would take an extraordinary amount of inner strength to allow them not to. And what is to be gained apart from isolation. The very interaction with others not only builds your understanding of the world around you and the people in it, but also can add meaning to your own life as well as a direction forward. Self-will and self-determination will only take you so far.

Man is a social being. Individuals survive and thrive through group interaction, group cohesiveness and a common cause that all promote a sense of belonging. Man, also seems programmed to try to make sense of his world. All these things have led to the rise of religions, laws, leadership and education. They are practical aspects that allow societies to function. An individual's free will to determine their own future can run at odds with the functioning of the society. That can cause conflict, but also growth of the individual and/or of the society as well. Sometimes the mere challenging of 'what is' can alter the 'what will be'. History often determines whether that is seen as good or bad, and, as explained before, history is merely a place marker in the time of the universe.

Nothing is predetermined when it comes within the times of birth and death of an individual. Life is fluid. Interactions come and go. People and societies are in a constant change of flux. Existentialists may argue that a person's individual will determines what happens. However, there are so many other factors involved in the pinball game of life that affect the will of people and their options and understanding of the options available to them. For some every day seems to have a number of crossroads to choose from, most of these intersections that there is no retuning to. What makes us choose one of the paths available to us? There are so many factors. Pinpointing one and attributing the title of free will to it, does not adequately represent the process. Nor does the ascribing of a god's will. Sometimes we don't know why because sometimes shit just happens. It is learning from the shit and the choices, that helps us be better prepared for the next fork in the road. It would be a bloody boring if there were no forks in the road or we kept on repeating the same mistakes.

Existentialism, in its truest form, doesn't fully explain how human's lives run their course. Religions don't either. Our lives are nor predetermined nor are they determined solely on one's own will. Choices we make are influenced by many things and in some cases choices don't exist. We have been programmed to choose life over death but even that can be overridden where the life can be seen as much worse than death. An individual's impact on the world and the universe is very much overrated. However, what they achieve in their life and how they affect those close to them should never be underestimated. For better or worse, the choices that they have made will influence and inform others, who will go on to influence and inform more people. The luckiest ones of us however, are those presented with an opportunity to not just exist, but to live their lives as fully as they can, and then choose to do so.

HOW DO WE ASSESS AND VALUE OUR USE OF TIME?

Time is merely a construct that has been created by humans based on a premise that things must travel in an orderly sequence and thus can be measured, recorded and reflected on. It follows a path that leads from birth to death, but one that is focused around the value of the length of time that a human lives. These lengths have been divided up into what appear to be spans based on humans' own planet's relationship with the closest objects nearby. Days were determined by Earth rotations. Years were counted by the number of orbits of the Earth around the sun. Months were originally calculations based on phases of the moon as were weeks. But these were arbitrary and fudging of mathematical formulae was necessary to ensure some sort of accuracy.

It is assumed that time is linear and that what has past will remain past and unchangeable. There has been no technology created yet by mankind's limited intelligence to alter that notion yet. What has once lived, has now irretrievably gone almost as if it had never existed. The only way that we know is through historical records and limited skills in palaeontology, geology, archaeology and studies of the theories of evolution. History speaks mainly of rulers, kings and queens and battles won and lost. It is also written by winners. The everyday person throughout history is lucky to get even a passing reference. But each and every person's life story is there frozen in some sort of amber, its secrets ready to be unlocked when tools become available. Mankind has made assumptions about time, its form, its length and the best use of it. Based on what is known now, that is understandable. Less than five hundred years ago scholars were arguing about how old the planet was and how long mankind itself had been in existence. Less than two hundred years ago, theories of evolution were just figments of imagination. Humans seem constrained by what they know, as if the garnering of knowledge is also linear. Their knowledge of time is based on the 'what has been will always be' mode of thinking that shackles all learning. Until something is proven to be one hundred and ten percent correct, it can't possibly be true. What if time is not linear but three or more dimensional and we have yet to figure out how to investigate it? Suddenly that makes everything that has ever been, or will be, inherently more valuable. Every person, every action and thought by them would seem to be of more worth and the intricate jigsaw of human existence more understandable even though it appears more complex. Perhaps a positive outcome of such awareness would be a greater tolerance of people as individuals.

To the mayfly which only has one or two days of life, every second matters. Humans with their longevity don't seem to make the most of the time they have being alive. Many end up with huge unachievable bucket lists at the end that may have been fulfilled if they had made better use of their time. However, that too is subjective and the best person to decide on whether a life has been well spent is the person who has lived it. What is critical is the maximising of the timespan an individual human has been allotted. That is where the value is best determined. Religions have promoted this concept for centuries, but have nearly all had an outside being determining the value of that individual's life. Perhaps this is to take away the difficulty and responsibility away from an individual or perhaps to establish control over a group of people. Self-assessment of one's own worth, given all the guilt that has been inculcated into us, is rarely productive. It can be very depressing because the guide a person has is their own interpretation of the world around them. That guide can be very narrow and dictated by limited experience and what has been indoctrinated. It can also be too broad and thus, overwhelming.

Although it can be neither bought nor sold, time is seen to very precious. We are told not to waste it and to use it wisely or we may run out of it. Yet logic states that it is a fixed mathematical amount which, depending on our circumstances, illogically appears to pass very slowly or very quickly. It is also one thing that theoretically can't be created nor destroyed. These seemingly strange contradictions are all to do with the way people view the quality of the time they have. And there lies the nub of the dilemma that people face. How do they assess their use of time? For many people, life involves surviving from one day to the next. They try to meet basic human needs and don't have the time and energy to reflect on what has been done and what could be. Their time has been allocated with little chance of free choice by them as it is determined by their surroundings and circumstances. For those in more so-called advanced societies whose basic needs are far more easily met, sometimes their difficulty lies in how to fill in time. They seek out entertainment to alleviate potential boredom and their society often promotes having time to do as many leisure activities as possible as this is good for stimulating an economy. People in these societies tend to gather experiences as they would material possessions. Are they better users of time than those who have a subsistence livelihood? It all comes down to the values that people believe in.

Some religions promote people's time on earth as a proving ground. Some look at it as just one experience that will be followed by another. Atheists see it as a once only opportunity that needs to be made the most of. These competing ideas challenge people. They confuse them simply because no-one knows what lies ahead in the future especially after a person dies. That one-way, linear view of time gives rise to much speculation, ignorance and conjecture. Until mankind develops ways to view accurately both forward and backward in time, nothing can be deemed to be certain as an explanation.

What if man's understanding of time and future technology allowed a person to replay and review in detail their own lives? It could be used as a prospectus, and current and past actions may be a good predictor of future outcomes. However, it may also lead to a stifling of creativity and people opting for the safe mode, especially if they believed that other people could also see what they were seeing. Would people shy away from the opportunity to be informed about themselves and prefer to be less self-aware? If a person's movement through time is linear and irreversible, then there is much to be gained from knowing more about themselves. Currently people are constrained by the rules of society and religion and some push back against these restrictions, not understanding the need for these. Being able to learn from your past actions is an important part of learning. Being able to examine choices made in the past, gives an opportunity for self-improvement throughout life, not just the brief reflective opportunity we are led to believe happens just before you die as your life passes before you. Even if the technology was available, could people handle what they saw, and would they have the time to view their life with the idea in mind that they could improve their lot? Would they instead just desire to go back and change things, without thinking that any change they may wish would impact on others?

If one assumes that an understanding of time and an improvement in technology would allow an audience capable of reviewing a person's life, then all sorts of possibilities and consequences may arise. Currently this is only the purview of a judgemental god or gods in various religions. Religions foster this notion to control their believers, but many societies have benefited from having a rigid structure and an outside unseen force as final arbiter. But what if anyone alive or perhaps even physically dead could play back not only their own life but also that of others? Would that change the behaviours of people? In a purely linear mode of time where time could not be altered once it had past, just the knowledge that your whole existence is being monitored all the time may impact upon freedom of speech, thought and action. People may play it safe and be unwilling to make mistakes. This could stifle so much creativity, discovery and progress. If it was possible for a person to play back any part of their life that had passed, would that impact on future decisions?

Exploring the concept of time itself and thinking outside of what the current understanding of what it is opens up a whole new field of opportunities. Mankind is so fixated on it and yet has not challenged the long-held beliefs of it. Is this because people are so reliant on knowing where they fit in in time and space? Is it because challenging those beliefs is also challenging known science and religious beliefs?

People seem content with the status quo. Time has become so much an ingrained part of a person's life. Life's journey is a high wire act and a linear view of time acts as a safety net. Remove it and fear of the unknown grows. However, that needs to be weighed up with the benefits achieved by improving people's understanding of where they fit in the vast universe's time and space.

HOW IMPORTANT ARE WE IN THE UNIVERSE?

(Look What I Found)

He was very young and possibly didn't know better. At least that's what the parents claimed. He found a bright shiny object on the ground. It was like a glowing marble. There seemed to be other marbles attached to it by invisible wires. The brightest marble was quite warm to touch and the little one decided that it must be alive. He carefully put it inside a clear case where you could see in but the thing inside couldn't see out. In case it was alive, he made sure that tiny little holes let the atmosphere in and a little bit of extra light. The strange objects seemed to hover in the container and he wondered whether it was upside down so he turned it over and made little holes on all sides, just in case. Very carefully he carried it home. He wondered what made the brightest marble glow. He wished he had a way of seeing each and every one of the marbles up very close as they might be alive or have tiny little creatures on them. He had no idea what the thing was that he had found, but it was quite colourful and the marbles were all different sizes. He watched carefully in the bright sunshine and wondered what it would be like in the container especially when you looked out. He was fascinated and watched intently and saw that some of the marbles changed position and seemed to spin.

His mother called him and he carefully carried the container. The sun was so bright and the three moons were high in the sky above his purple planet. He showed his mum and said that he liked the tiny blue marble the best even though it wasn't the biggest. She pointed to the tiny little dot near it saying that it had a little friend.

In another place where two suns seemed to glow in the sky, a little girl found a similar object and too put it in a clear container with holes in it. Her favourite marble was the purple one with the three dots attached. She wondered if perhaps there were tiny little creatures living on the surface of that purple marble.

On a significantly larger planet, a creature found an object that was made of two glowing balls surrounded by many tiny darker ones……………….

Meanwhile on a tiny blue planet locked away in a very small container, a young child was called by his mother to stop playing with his toy microscope and come and look at the Russian babushka dolls his grandmother had just arrived with.

CHOOSING MY RELIGION

What are the consequences of having the wrong religion? Is there such a thing as the wrong religion? Many people are raised to believe that there is only one true religion and those that don't follow it are pagans who will be condemned to some sort of hell. They may have had little choice as to their beliefs. Never being exposed to the true one, being totally indoctrinated by their parents and the society that they live in; should that consign them to damnation?

In essence since humans began to wonder about the world around them, religion has been created to explain the unknown. There are two other functions it performs. It helps engender a social code of ethics that enables humans to live together in a framework of rules and laws. It also tries to deal with fear of dying that humans carry with them because humans have been blessed with a brain capable of questioning their own existence.

Myths and legends grew out of the unknown. Every religion has them, has always had them. Simple rudimentary explanations about common things such as stars, why food may be scarce, illness and why men and women are different, were passed down from generation to generation and remained relatively unquestioned by many even when provable evidence of a different explanation was found. Often these stories were deemed sacrosanct and formed the basis of religious movements. Some zealots would rather dismiss reality than go against what had been passed down to them. As new discoveries are made, they are made to conform into the pre-existing dogma or are dismissed entirely. The latter is quite obvious when related to science, in particular medicine. Despite the inherent fear of dying, going against religious beliefs may be more daunting.

Mankind is a social group of creatures. Whether this is because primitive man realised that strength lies in numbers or whether we are pre-programmed that way is debatable. To be able to operate as a society, rules and customs are essential. Given the free thinking and independent nature of mankind, an overlay of explanation is important. Religion has provided that. The rulers of groups in the past relied on their medicine men, their sorcerers, their priests to justify the actions that were being taken. The mystique that accompanied these people enabled them to be rarely challenged. They became the bearers of all knowledge, the explainers of the unknown and as powerful, if not more powerful, than the rulers of the society. They were as venerated as much as the religion themselves. As such, they were the go-to person of a tribal group which occasionally set them at odds with the ruling class. In many religions they were supposedly the conduit between normal people and the "gods" that had been created to explain why things occurred. One myth reinforced another.

These myths originally were handed down by word of mouth. They were often based around people and events and so had some legitimacy as far as those who heard them believed. Eventually written word took over and that further legitimised them because the uneducated illiterate viewed such documentation as indisputable.

The danger came to these carriers of truth when someone questioned what had occurred. This would often cause sects to generate based on disagreements of certain understandings. Some would hold true to the written word even though it was no longer plausible given what had been learned over the years. Some absorbed new ideas, recognised that some of what they had based their religion on was improbable and described these elements as parables and stories written to prove a point.

These sects were merely sub-groups of an all-encompassing religion and at times reinforced and spread the religion's basic beliefs further unifying a group, enabled the exile of unbelievers and radicals, suppressed women and reinforced the ruling class. It may not have been the most logical way of organising a society, but it worked. Each religion believed that they were the one true religion and others who supported a different religion needed to be converted or have their religion destroyed or debunked. Animosity between religious groups was rife.

One consequence of such a unified group was its exploitation by those in power whose level of greed was strong. Tithes and taxes were linked to religious beliefs. Wars created by greed were justified through religion. There were often two arms of power, the secular and the religious, and both amassed wealth, controlled knowledge and often worked hand in glove with each other. Trade brought in new ideas, some of which had to be quashed, but it also brought in opportunities to expand territory and religious influence. Not all religious wars nor missionary practices were motivated by the desire that the ignorant needed to be converted.

When religions are distilled down to their basic elements, they are remarkably the same in many aspects. They provide the fundamental notions by which a society can function. Most preach against violence and murder. They advocate the recognition of the ownership of property. They promote the care of the young, the elderly and those in need. They support the family as being an underpinning structure within society. These basic tenets are then dressed up in words and rituals peculiar to a particular religion, thus bringing in a mystical quality that cements the bonds between those who advocate a religious belief and the practice of a society. It is often the rituals that differentiate different forms of religion that are highlighted and used to decry another religion and seek to destroy it. One wonders what would happen if such rituals and the lofty positions those that practice them were held in, were swept aside. Would going back to basic social canons be more beneficial for a society? Would people become more caring, sharing and supportive of others if a far simpler social framework was in place?

Mankind has been saddled with the knowledge that death is inevitable and the fear of death is all pervading because we wonder about life, thinking, "Is that all there is?" Yet it is the fear of death that makes us want to remain alive and makes the short time on Earth worth living. Death has been seen as final, yet religions have exploited the question that each person has to face at some time,

"What happens next?" The concept of an afterlife exists in most religions, whether it be in the form of reincarnation, a heaven, or that the body may have died but an inner part or spirit lives on. Tied in with this is that a value judgement is placed on how you have lived your life and you will be rewarded or punished accordingly. This leverage is used to help people conform to basic social rules.

It is the not knowing that is one motivator that drives people towards accepting a particular religion. An explanation is given and, although it might seem ludicrous, is accepted. This has been reinforced by centuries of mysticism and ownership by religious entities of knowledge. A lie told often enough can become a truth, is an old saying; but is what a religion promotes as an afterlife, a lie? At present, their explanation can't be either proven or disproved. However, due to the various representations of an afterlife by different religions and each religion's total belief that they are correct, millions of people are going to be disappointed if indeed there is an afterlife. Some will be condemned to rot in hell because they were not of the correct faith according to some explanations of death. The concept of a heaven and a hell is also preached heavily, but is that to force people to conform to social mores, or do they really exist? Those who advocate a particular religious belief appear absolutely sure, but the one real truth is that no-one knows.

As mankind's understanding of the world around it has increased, particularly with the aid of science, what has become more apparent is, that instead of discovering the reasons for our existence, we have found that there is so much we have yet to learn as to where we fit in the universe and across time. Religions have offered us explanations in the past and they may continue to do so in the future. One of the things that may happen is that old religious models will be seen as anachronistic and no longer valid. The basic elements will still be there but the frippery and rituals may be gone. Instead of highlighting the differences between religious beliefs and disparaging them, maybe there will be a time of enlightenment where a greater understanding of what they have in common will occur. We may be able to accept that there are things that we don't understand and be content that that will always be the case. That would mean that fanciful explanations from the past may not be held as firmly, if at all. It would also mean that the choice of religion becomes less critical and belief may be focused around the benefits to be gained by working together in a sharing and supportive social structure regardless of race, colour, gender or creed.

HOW TO ARGUE

Around us we witness arguments between people who believe that one person is right and the other person is therefore wrong. Can both be right and both be wrong? It depends on the level of understanding of each of them. People confuse knowledge with intelligence, and intelligence with understanding. A person's understanding of a situation depends on their experiences, their education and their beliefs. Everyone has different levels of these and therefore, based on these, people can believe themselves to be right even against an argument put up by someone else that has factual evidence supporting it. Confronting these people and downplaying their understanding is not the way to extend their experiences, education and beliefs. It is more likely to lock them into what they have. No-one has the complete understanding of everything and therefore everyone's understanding has some validity to themselves.

To argue successfully, you need a greater understanding of the person who is holding different views and where they are coming from. You need to accept their views as being important to them, just as much as yours are important to you. You must be willing to change your own views, because how can you expect others to change theirs if you are unwilling to change your own. New information is being found every day and not all of it may be correct, or your understanding of it may not be correct. Science is based on what we know and science also looks for what we don't know. Beliefs, including those expressed in religion, are what we use often to explain what we don't know. As more information comes to light, beliefs change if people feel in a safe place to take that information on board. Thrusting it down someone else's throat is not making them feel safe.

Knowing more does not mean that you are correct all the time. If you choose to criticise the person and his/her beliefs, you will not induce change. If you provide evidence for them to think about and perhaps adapt into their own knowledge bank and into their beliefs, they may change when they are ready. People learn at different rates. They come from different backgrounds. They have had different experiences. Their right to have an opinion is as important as your own. You don't have to agree with them.

Trying to quash their opinions because "you know better" may seem the right thing to do. Sometime in the future you will be challenged with new ideas and new information and if you have your own fixed, locked-in opinions then you may have difficulty taking on anything new. An argument should not be all about someone winning and someone losing, or one person showing off their intellect. It is an opportunity for all those participating to learn new things and increase their understanding of themselves and of others.

ETHICS – A Discussion Paper

CONTENTS

- Introduction

- What are ethics

- How does our brain function?

- When and how are ethics formed?

- What factors influence the formation of ethics?

- Why aren't everyone's ethics the same?

- Why are ethics flexible and what may cause a change in ethics?

- What do you do when you are faced with an ethical dilemma?

Introduction

To be caught in an ethical dilemma is to be bound by a set of self-imposed views. These views are built up over a period of time and often that when the length of time is longer, the more difficult the issue is. We are not born with a sense of right and wrong. That comes from our interaction with the world around us, particularly the people around us. There is no inbuilt fear of anything when we are born. That makes us very vulnerable and therefore we need protection and to gain an understanding of what we need to be protected from. Dangers surround us and we are taught or learn to recognise them. Tasting, touching and observing give us clues as to what is good and what is bad for us from the get go. How our body reacts and informs our brain which then causes the body to react in certain circumstances. We store that information and use it for further exploration of the world around us. In basic animalistic terms, such reactions can induce a fight or flight response. We can passively accept what is happening around us or react in some way. That is determined by what we have learned along the way.

Just as what we put in our memory bank, our thought processes themselves can be shaped. Our brain has different modes of learning. Different processes are used to interpret the information we garner. Knowledge is slotted into previously acquired knowledge and connections are made so that we can make sense of new information and experiences. Sometimes more of those can lead to greater understanding. Sometimes however, it can be overwhelming and cause us to question previous understandings. Challenging what we have understood to be unassailable truths is extremely difficult. It is a massive shock to the system, creates confusion and causes the need for a higher order thinking pattern. Often our inability to cope with such challenging notions can cause us to dismiss the new information and make us revert back to and entrench earlier truths. Some perfect examples in history were the belief that the world was flat and that evolution never occurred. There are still people who refuse to accept the science that proves those beliefs to be false. Does that make them wrong? Does that make them ignorant and stupid? No, it means that the 'truths' they have learned earlier on in their lives are so fixed that they cannot or will not adapt to new information. It may also mean that the people who taught them those original ideas, in their minds, can never be questioned or must be respected. When someone you are in awe of tells you something, it appears to carry far more weight. Parents, teachers, ministers of religion are in incredible positions of power and influence, possibly more than they know. With very tractable children, students and followers, they should be aware of their responsibility to allow divergent views and permit questioning of beliefs. However, they too are bound by what they have learned and been taught along their own life's journey.

Unless we have an open and accepting mind, when we are confronted with ideas that challenge preconceived notions, we are likely to fall into the basic animal responses. We will gather with likeminded people because there is strength and protection in numbers. We will choose to run and hide from the ideas presented to us. We will fight against them, sometimes physically but often through words. We weaponise the language we use and at times ignore logic completely, as being rational may be counterproductive. The point at which we find we have to make choices is what we call an ethical dilemma.

A child having learned some basic rights and wrongs either self-taught or by others, encounters dilemmas all the time. Exploration of their world poses risks and rewards along the way. Only by trying things they actually learn. Faced with unknowns and temptations, they can be less risk averse than adults. Their cause-and-effect understandings of consequences is nowhere near as refined and understood. Often their parents desire to protect their child; wrapping them up in cotton wool, can inhibit the child's learning. Mistakes need to be made so new information can be adapted into previous understandings. Choosing how much risk their child should be exposed to is a constant concern for parents. Ensuring there is a safety net to catch the child when they fall helps development far more than straight out forbidding of doing something. Being forbidden from doing something can make that thing more tantalising and create a desire where there may have been none. Parents have to make choices and often those choices are coloured by the way that they have been raised. Most of the time their only experience and understanding of parenting comes from how they were parented. That is a very limited set of knowledge that is interpreted subjectively.

As right and wrong are also very subjective constructs, developing one's own set of values is difficult and is different for everyone. Social mores are passed down from generation to generation. Many are often rebelled against at some point. Often, they are flexible and are adapted as society as a whole learns more. Different societies have different socially accepted norms and this can cause conflict both internally and externally. Mankind has a tendency to want to change things into one homogenised way of thinking, believing and behaving. Being outside the norm is frowned upon and people are often cast out because they think, behave and are different. That doesn't mean that the majority prevail. More often than not, the rich and powerful prevail and at times throughout history we have seen societies blossom or stagnate ideologically because of those things. We have had the Dark Ages and the Renaissance as good examples. We have had societies made extinct by others that thought they knew better. Being different doesn't mean being wrong. The challenge that exists is for us to find tolerance and acceptance.

The concepts of right and wrong are drivers of religion. Religions are used to provide a social framework and to make some sense of the world. They are not necessarily logical and rational. Because they are so entrenched in learnings gained in the past, they are so incredibly slow to adapt to more modern understandings. Over time they have become less relevant because of this lack of adaptability.

At the same time, they have become a refuge for some people. Zealots abound though and they can turn would-be followers off. Although many religions have similar teachings, many followers believe that there can only be one religion and are unwilling to tolerate or accept any other. In the past and even today that has led to isolationism and war. At the heart of the issue is the lack of understanding of the subjectivity of right and wrong.

Right and wrong are learnt early in one's life. By the age of seven most people have a sense of values that they will carry with them through life. They will modify and adapt them, but the core values will remain unless something very dramatic happens. Religion, ethics and social mores therefore have their greatest effect on the very young. It is imperative that children not be indoctrinated but allowed to develop their own understandings. Any ethical dilemma they face should be about their own ethics rather than someone else's.

Chapter 1

What are ethics?

Ethics have been defined as the set of moral principles and values that govern a person's behaviour or the conducting of an activity. As humans at birth do not come with a built-in set of ethics just the capacity to eventually develop them, ethics are almost entirely influenced by the environment around them and the interaction with it. Ethics are not a survival attribute similar to the automatic responses of breathing and the beating of a heart. Nor are they part of a secondary survival set which covers the basic needs of eating, drinking, warmth clothing and seeking shelter. They are not intrinsic actions like fight and flight responses. They are way beyond the need for comforting, social interaction and activity. Although they are good tools to make those things easier.

There is a difference too between an outside imposed set of ethics and ones that are created or adapted and owned by an individual. As we mature, we gradually move from the outside imposed ones to the ones we develop as our own. There is no set age when the latter occurs but as it needs a higher order of thinking which occurs in the frontal lobe of the brain, the last part of the brain to fully develop; it is logical to assume that would not occur before adolescence.

Outside imposed ethics are ones that are determined by a social structure, be it your family, a group that you belong to, or a much broader society. It may be a combination of these and often these have cross fertilisation of ethics and occasional lashes. These groups have codes of behaviour that it is expected that you will adhere to. Sometimes these codes are unspoken. There are often consequences for your adherence or non-adherence to these codes of behaviour.

The ones that an individual creates or adapts from others, but are self-imposed, are rarely written down. They are internalised and can have a big influence on a person's behaviour. These ethics are highly individualised and quite complex. As such, no two people will have the same set of ethics, simply because no two people will have had exactly the same interaction with the environment around them. To understand more fully how ethics are formed, we need to understand a little more about the brain, how it functions and how it develops.

Chapter 2

How does our brain function?

The brain is not made simply of one mass of tissue that fires electrical messages through synapses. It is composed of many separate but interconnected and interrelated sections that are responsible for different functions. Without such order, the amount of information collected, collated and retrieved would overwhelm it and the brain functionality would slow down immensely. Evidence can be found supporting the separate functionality in the responses of people who have had head trauma or strokes. Many lose control of certain functions or have a deterioration of what they were previously capable of doing.

Most people refer the cerebral cortex as being the brain but the whole brain involves much more than that. The brain is made up of many parts The cerebral cortex is divided into two hemispheres These two hemispheres appear in all mammals and allow the better and quicker use of the brain's capacity. They also allow for damage to be repaired to the brain while the body can still function. There is a link between the two hemispheres called the corpus callosum and each hemisphere has four lobes that grow at different times and at different rates.

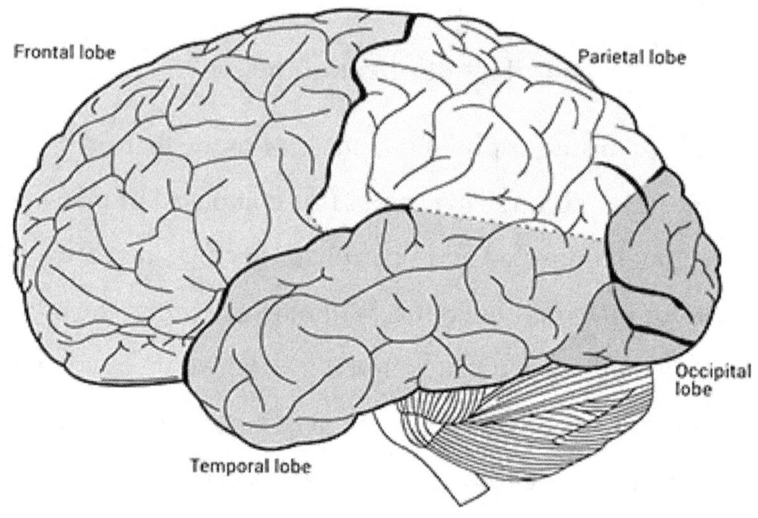

Image Source: https://qbi.uq.edu.au/brain/brain-anatomy/lobes-brain

(With kind permission from The Queensland Brain Institute)

Each of the lobes and the cerebellum (which is yet another part of the brain) have different functions:

The **frontal lobe** is involved in personality characteristics, decision-making and movement. It also assists with speech and the sense of smell.

The **parietal lobe** helps us to identify objects and understand where our body is in relation to objects around us. It is also involved in interpreting pain and touch in the body and helps the brain understand spoken language.

The **occipital lobe** is involved with vision.

The **temporal lobe** is involved in short-term memory, speech, musical rhythm and some degree of smell recognition.

The **cerebellum** has the function of coordinating voluntary muscle movements and helps us to maintain posture, balance and equilibrium. It is believed that it is also involved in thought, emotions and social behaviour.

Various glands and organs lie within the brain and they have different functions.

The **pituitary gland** oversees the function of other glands in the body. It also regulates the flow of hormones from the thyroid, adrenals, ovaries and testicles

The **hypothalamus** controls the pituitary gland. It also regulates body temperature, sleep patterns, hunger and thirst responses and also is involved in memory and emotion.

The **amygdala** regulate emotion and memory They are involved with with the brain's reward system, stress, and the "fight or flight" response when we feel threatened.

The **hippocampus organ** receives data from the cerebral cortex and uses it to assist with memory, how we learn, how we find our way and our locational bearings.

The **pineal gland** is located deep in the brain. It responds to light and dark and secretes melatonin which regulates physical, mental, and behavioural changes involved in a daily cycle including sleep patterns.

The image below gives a rough idea of the functions of the various parts of the brain. You will notice that the heart rate and breathing section is at the lower part of the skull in the most protected area of the head.

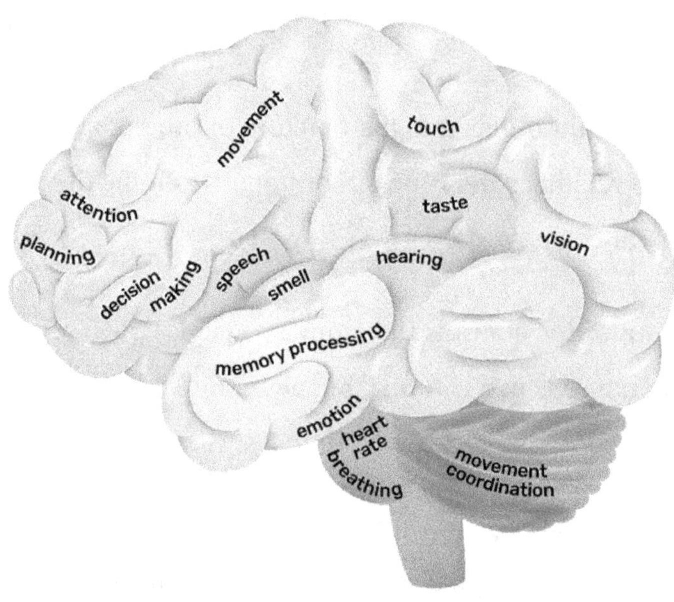

Image Source: https://qbi.uq.edu.au/brain/brain-anatomy/lobes-brain

(With kind permission from The Queensland Brain Institute)

Humans have evolved over millions of years and it is believed that the various sections of the brain have changed as well, based on the needs required. Core automatic functions have remained much the same but other areas have begun developing earlier and have become more dominant as the environment around has changed. Events such as the introduction of the printing press and with it the much wider dissemination of information, the growth in educational institutions may have forced the brain to adapt and grow in different ways. Indeed, longitudinal studies are now being conducted on the effect of digital technology.

One section of the brain that grows the slowest is the portion of the frontal lobe that is involved in higher order thinking. This section is where self-discipline, social morality and ethical considerations are established, reviewed and modified. Arguably there is no reason for it to develop earlier. These are more adult concepts and are based on life experience. They are formed by observation, participation and a contest of ideas. While young children are taught and expected to know right from wrong and to have self-discipline, their responses are often more Pavlovian than with a full understanding. They are merely following the teachings of others around them rather than making their own judgements. Because their frontal lobe has not fully developed to the point where they are making rational decisions based on their own experiences, this type of learning allows them to be manipulated to conform to other people's standards and expectations.

Chapter 3

When and how are ethics formed?

To understand how ethical dilemmas occur, it is important to understand how we learn because ethical dilemmas occur when there is a confusion caused when new information causes us to question previous beliefs of what is right and what is wrong.

A child in the womb has all its needs met through its lifeline, the umbilical cord. It is surrounded by a protective layer, the amniotic sac and it has only one purpose and that is to grow and develop physically. Little is known about the growth of the brain during this time. It does grow but how it functions is speculation. It is thought that as all it needs to do is to focus on growth, survival and development, the brain doesn't need to function at any higher level. Its growth depends upon genetic issues, illnesses and the quality of what it receives through the umbilical cord. Abnormalities can occur because of these factors but are difficult to accurately assess until after the child is born unless those abnormalities are quite severe.

It would be unreasonable to think that some higher order thought processes were happening as that might be counterproductive to the birthing process. The birth of a child is one of the most traumatic experiences it will ever have. It has been nurtured on average for 40-42 weeks. It has in most cases had all its needs met. It hasn't had to breathe, swallow food or have any of its senses challenged. Yet as it is born, it feels pain for the first time. It has to suck in air into its tiny lungs. All its senses kick in and it is in a totally foreign environment. Its food and life support system has literally been cut off. A brain functioning above survival mode would have probably fought against leaving the womb and made the birthing more difficult. It would have been unable to cope with all the inputs of the new environment and thus affected the innate automatic functions of breathing and needing sustenance and warmth. It is hard to believe that humans have evolved in such a way that being born might jeopardise their survival.

The brain needs to function at a level that is required at the time. For the first few months, a child needs to sleep, eat and excrete. Gradually receptors come on line. It recognises food sources. It recognises care and comfort. It learns that a cry will bring those things and that it can use different cries to indicate different needs. Its senses become more alert and able to distinguish differences. All these are gradual steps and one piece of knowledge gained helps build others. That process is lifelong; but as it is often described it literally is baby steps.

Neuroscientists have over the years come to learn more about the various functions of the brain, of its separate but interconnected parts, how it grows in size and capacity to do many things, how it declines in performance as we age or as it becomes diseased or injured. This neuroplasticity allows people to deal with the environment around them, try to make some sense of it and to adapt to it. It demonstrates the reason why people think differently over time and think differently to others. The brain receives an enormous number of inputs. It organises those in such a way that the important ones can be recalled quickly. It constructs neural pathways to store and retrieve information based on the links it makes between those pieces of information. From birth we are exposed to an increasing number of sensations, observations and experiences. These become the foundation blocks of a very complex association of ideas which build on each other so that we can gain an understanding of and a reaction to the world around us.

Basic automatic functions such as breathing, using our senses, organ functioning etc. kick in, if not in the womb, then at birth itself. From there higher order functions are developed through exposure to the environment around us. Initially the responses to inputs from our senses of sight, hearing, taste, touch and smell can be categorised three basic ways - good, bad and indifferent. These can trigger basic fight, flight and do-nothing responses. However, the human brain gradually builds up a database of these sensations and creates much finer distinctions between good, bad and indifferent. It also learns to find links between the sensations from different senses and trigger different responses to those inputs. In a newborn child the automatic function of the body needing sustenance is to cry. When food is provided, it doesn't need to think about sucking, its mouth does it automatically. However, it learns to associate the provision of food with the source and identifies with that source. It knows who that source is after a short period of time, by the smell, the taste, the sound, the sight and the feel of that source. It can distinguish between sources. Its brain has already begun a higher order of functioning. A response is triggered beyond just the automatic sucking motion. The data has been compiled and analysed and a bond between the source and the child has begun. This is one of the earliest signs of development. It shows that there is an awareness growing. Of course, this later on can lead to rejection of types of food that is offered which can be a source of annoyance for parents and a game for children, but this too shows brain development.

That is just one example of a very complex response to inputs from a child's immediate environment. The speed at which that data is absorbed analysed synthesised and responded to is incredible. That speed and the responses themselves provide markers for brain growth development but as everyone's brain and environment are different, the markers are arbitrary and offer only a vague way of comparison. If any one of the senses is compromised or indeed excels that changes the inputs and brain functioning. Exposure to information or experiences can determine how much data is stored and the way links are made. Over-stimulation of the senses can be as constricting as under-stimulation. Both these points are applicable all throughout a person's life.

Every person's brain is different, develops differently and functions differently. Some of that is because of genetics and some of that is because the brain is an active receptacle of information gained which is then stored, cross matched and used when necessary. Scientists have nominated certain age markers as to brain development and decline. These are arbitrary and there will be people who don't fall into those categories for one reason or another. These markers are only guidelines as neuroplasticity is different for every individual. Because the brain functions by building on inputs and finding links between data gathered it is in the very early years that the markers are truest and more observable. If observable behaviour responses in a very young child fall outside those markers, then that could be a clue that there may be a physiological or neurological issue. It may be that one or more of the senses is heightened or not functioning as it should. It may be some issue to do with the brain itself. Early intervention may be required and may have long term benefits. However, it may be because the child is progressing at its own individual rate. The older a child becomes the broader the differences appear between children because the data input and the linking of the data is more varied. While the experiences for children may be similar, how they are interpreted could be vastly different based on previous experiences and how their brain sorts the data input. Unfortunately, adults tend to want to homogenise so many things and expectations and teaching are often solely focused around a norm rather than a recognition that all children are different from day one and will grow and develop in their own way at their own rate.

Continual repetition of actions leads to higher speeds along neural pathways. Inputs that are regular and consistent help to make responses seem to become more and more automatic. This is essentially what is behind rote learning. Just as physical responses are conditioned into muscle memory, so too can thought responses be trained the same way. This can be observed in the rehabilitation of stroke and head trauma patients where what were once almost automatic responses have to be slowly relearned. In young children regularly used connections come to the fore while others are put to the back of mind so to speak or disappear as the brain develops. The amount of sensory data that is available is far more than a developing brain can take in and use and therefore the brain is forced to seek the most important and discard the possible irrelevant. A one-off piece of information that has no practical application or requires no action is often left by the wayside. This process continues throughout people's lives. They may have déjà vu moments if the information appears at some later point, but often the thought has been lost.

In learning, retention of knowledge used to receive the highest priority, but it is now realised that the amount of knowledge available is overwhelming and so the ability to seek out and use required appropriate knowledge is deemed to be far more important. Teaching practice has now caught up with scientific understanding of how the brain works. There is a place for rote learning, but what is learned by that method will be retained longer by practical application. The same can be said of being shown how to do something. If it is merely observed and there is no active participation then retention is far more difficult and unlikely. The old adage "I hear and I forget, I see and I remember, I do and I understand" has solid foundation.

More abstract notions are difficult to grasp. Children learn through experimentation and experience. This trial-and-error approach so necessary in many aspects has its shortcomings in abstract ideas. When questioned why they should do or not do something, they are quite likely to simply say because it was not right to do otherwise. Their definition of what is right and wrong at such an early age is nor usually their own. It is what they have been told by their parents, their teachers or their community. Many respond unthinkingly and unquestioningly. It is only as they get older that their minds challenge the reasons for their expected responses.

Within any group, common organised thought helps to both unify and control people. It can stifle individual differences and isolate those who are different. As a social being, having some sort of structure is important and is comforting. Most young children learn quickly how to fit in. They learn not to challenge ideas especially those espoused by their elders and/or those more powerful. To do so risks isolation, physical and/or emotional punishment and non-acceptance. Their minds and bodies are not ready to stand alone. To establish what the rules are, they push boundaries, not as acts of defiance as such, but more to find out what is and isn't acceptable. What they find is that those boundaries are flexible depending on the time and mood of the person imposing those boundaries. They find that not all people are the same when it comes to what the rules are and how they are applied. These differences at first may confuse them, but they do add to their knowledge. They learn that people can think differently and they also learn to play the system. Both of which are good things to know as they go through life.

For most, the terrible twos, and the tantrum threes are where they learn basic boundaries. There is more passivity from then on which makes the formal education of school set at the right time. They enter with an innate desire to learn at a critical moment of their development. The period between the ages of four and seven years of age generally set them up for life both academically and socially. Aristotle's quote "Give me a child until he is seven and I will show you the man" is well founded. We see that in our schools. Basic concepts in science, arts, mathematics and language are best taught in the early years of schooling as they are retained better and become the building blocks for all that follows. The same can be said for behaviours and attitudes.

The period of adolescence, from the ages of ten through to nineteen approximately, sees a massive change in young people both physically, mentally and socially. Behaviours change. If they have had good grounding in their socialisation skills they learn quicker to adapt to these changes. Once again, they are in a phase of pushing boundaries so that they can establish their own identity. They question, they challenge and they adapt to the responses they receive. Preconceived determinations of right and wrong come under scrutiny by them and it is in this period for most where lifelong owned personalised ethics are established. Their brains frontal lobe has grown enough to accommodate and manage the conflict of ideas that will establish those ethics. Many adolescents will question their past learned definitions of right and wrong and may agree to retain them. For others it is very confronting to find that they can't agree with what they have learnt. Outward passivity can be used to mask inward turmoil. Adolescence is a period where individual identity is being established and is yet another critical phase in a person's life. They are more aware of the world around them and are trying to establish not only where they fit in but also how they fit in. This is a period where they develop and confirm a set of ethics that for the most part they will carry throughout their lives.

Chapter 4

What factors influence the formation of ethics?

Young children's understanding of what are the social rules and regulations is at a level where they are told and shown what to do. Their ability to understand why is not developed fully. They follow the rules because there are often negative consequences if they don't. It is not for most children a moral decision. Society has developed constraints on behaviours mostly for good reasons but the reasons are not easily explained to children.

Religious beliefs are often taught through rote learning and the development of faith in the abstract is a long-term process. Moral conditioning takes place, parables are told, rituals are participated in, songs are sung because the abstract is difficult to teach and even harder to understand particularly by the young whose brains are not developed enough to handle it. They may be taught morals and ethics but whether they understand them at their age is a moot point. The question has been asked many times about the teaching of religion. "Are we really just brainwashing our children?"

Genetic factors influence brain growth and development. There are arguments regarding how much genetic predisposition influences brain functionality and whether social conditioning although alters any pre-determined factors. The brain is an organ of the body and other organs have genetic influencers, therefore it would seem logical to assume that the brain is no different. The same can be said for social factors, particularly when it comes to things requiring higher order thinking such as the development of creative thinking and development of ethics and morals. The belief that certain groups of people were born morally corrupt has more to do with racism than scientific fact. In fact, there is far more evidence to prove that moral corruption is a learned behaviour than one that is genetically embedded in an individual. Children learn by observing the actions of people around them. They imitate and replicate the behaviours of their parents, peers and role models. Moral judgements are made by others of them, but it is not until they develop their own sense of values, that they make judgements about their own behaviours. This is recognised in the area of law where age is a consideration as to whether a person is indeed responsible for their own actions. Different societies have different social constructs and adolescents develop their own ethics based around the society they grow up in. There is no one set of ethics that fits all across the world or even within a family as an ethical framework is formed from life experiences and understandings, and everyone's is individual. Like generally will seek like in social situations and groupings of adolescents tend to have like-minded individuals in them. This is critical when it comes to the development of a set of values. The comparison and contrast within a group helps to confirm or reject principles. There is fluidity within these groupings as individuals find conflicts with or agreements with principles held by others.

It can be argued that ethics are developed much earlier than adolescence and that children generally have a pretty fair idea of what is right or wrong. However, ethics are more than the knowledge of right and wrong. To be able to act ethically you need to be able to actively choose to do the right thing without any outside influence. You have to have determined yourself what is right and what is wrong and nor be influenced by others. That way you both own the ethics and you own the actions that you take. Those ethics are not ones that are imposed on you. During adolescence as you develop independence from your parents or guardians, your sense of values that you have been raised to accept is challenged and questioned. Without going through that process, you may not actually own those ethics. If you maintain the same ethics after that process, they are then yours. Many people do not vary from the way that they were raised but that doesn't mean that they are not independent thinkers. They have made decisions and accepted their choices. For a lot of adolescents, they may not consciously know that they are developing a set of ethics. In fact, the whole concept may seem foreign to them. Being able to justify their decisions and actions is a sign that they have an internalised sense of values. There will be some who never question the set of morals and principles that have been put in place for them. They may just blindly accept them or not have the mental capacity to do that. The human brain is designed to receive information, process it and then determine appropriate responses to it. It builds upon past knowledge, with new information. If there is no new information, then what is there becomes a truth. The danger in such a situation is that young impressionable people are not exposed to new ideas and never learn to question what they have been told. The effect is that they adopt the ethics of others. It is how cults work. It is the way some religions work. Blind obedience to someone else's rules stifles the opportunities for higher order thinking. Brains need new information to maintain neural networks, to continue to grow and develop. Over time a brain's functionality will naturally decline and will be unable to take in new data and process it effectively. Although many societies, governments and religions may find it much easier to maintain control by limiting information, not allowing questioning of 'truths' and by stifling responses, they are doing a disservice to the young and the future of their society. If people are not permitted to ask why or why not, how can progress be made?

There's a vast array of ethical considerations for people to choose from so that they can manage their own lives. If that range is limited, their lives are managed by others. Just like very young children test boundaries, adolescents and adults need to test boundaries so that they can understand where they fit in the world. Constrain them too tightly and they will rebel. Give them absolute freedom to do as they please, then they will become lost. Teach them that they have rights but also responsibilities and they will have a framework and a reference point to develop their own sense of self and their own underlying ethics. Society will shape them. Their genetics will shape them. The people they come in contact with will shape them. But they need to be the ones who shape themselves the most or life could become a very hollow and ultimately a very unsatisfying existence.

Chapter 5

Why aren't everyone's ethics the same?

If we accept the premise that a person's self-imposed ethics are determined by environmental rather than genetic factors, should we dismiss genetic factors entirely. They can determine how we interact with the environment we grow up in. Someone who is predisposed to a different level of athleticism than others will be viewed differently in most societies and thus will respond accordingly. The same will apply to many genetic factors which have often determined a person's ancestors place in society and therefore inevitably their own.

One of the biggest determinants of ethics involves a combination of wealth, privilege and position within a society. Those who have it tend to have a different sort of upbringing and a different sort of education. They are surrounded by people and groups with different sorts of ethics that get absorbed into the ones the take on as their own later in life. Position in society of parents definitely is a factor that changes the immediate environment for young children. It often narrows the group of people they associate with as they grow up and therefore narrows their exposure to a wide range of ideas and experiences.

Education is supposed to be the biggest opportunity to change a person's status, yet, because education levels and opportunities are still very much related to one's existing position in society, few actually make that significant break away from the sort of environment that their parents had. Even if they do gain social mobility, they carry with them the experience-based views that they have been exposed to at a young age. Education does not wipe the slate clean. Going home from a school that exposes you to a wide range of ideas and ideals, to a place that has contradictory or very much narrowed views sews confusion among young children.

Young children who struggle to have basic needs met will have different experiences and a different outlook than ones who have nearly every need and desire met.

Children who are exposed to a wide range of enriching experiences will probably form different ethics long term to those who don't have those experiences.

Children who grow up in a supportive family and community will have a different outlook on life than those who aren't as fortunate.

Exposure to religious teachings influence the internalised ethics of an individual. That can have good, but also bad consequences depending on the doctrines, the delivery and the flexibility of the religion. While most religions have similar moral beliefs in them, many of these teachings are shrouded in historical contexts that people find difficult to understand. Parables used to help explain things can cause confusion. If emphasis is placed on certain aspects of a religion other than the core elements, those core elements can fall by the wayside. A young child is often caught between what they know to be true from their experience and what the religion is telling them to be true. Who do they believe? The person in a position of power and influence or their own understandings?

The same sorts of choices have to be made if there is conflict of understanding caused by parents, friends, social groups etc. Children are wanting to fit in. They are wanting to be accepted. They are constantly being told that they don't know enough about the world to make such decisions, so they bury these conflicts inside or dismiss them entirely. Rarely do they rebel successfully against those outside more powerful influences. As their experience grows, their desire for independence grows, their understanding of the world around them improves and their brain is able to cope with higher order thinking, they then are more likely to stand their ground and rebel. Welcome to the teenage years.

Other people's perception of a person is also another variable that influences a person's set of ethics. In most cases children will adapt to suit those perceptions. Indeed, many adults do. It is part of an ongoing desire for acceptance. These perceptions and the adherence of an individual to them can dictate what that person becomes, how they act, who they associate with and ultimately their belief system. A flippant comment by someone they respect may hinder their own personal growth.

Role models that people are exposed to can be very influential in how a person behaves and what they think of themselves. Children often latch on to ideals of what they aspire to. Initial role models of their parents broaden as they meet or see others with attributes, possessions or a lifestyle that appeals. Promotion of role models through the vast array of media available today is rife and children have a many and varied group of role models to choose from. Some may be very good influences and some the opposite. Often children aren't shown the complete picture of their chosen role model, merely an artificial portrayal of that person. Just as children are not taught how to assess validity of information they come across; they are also nor taught how to answer why there is a need to accurately assess the projected images of their "heroes". This can give them unrealistic expectations and cloud their thinking about their ongoing development of what is wrong and what is right which will form the basis of the ethics that they will develop.

These are just a few elements that influence children along the way. They also have an impact on revision by adults of their own ethics.

The sort of environment that people grow up in, the type of education they have, the people they meet are significant factors. As all these will be different for everyone, it would be very unrealistic to expect people's ethics to be exactly identical. Even then, if they were, people are so individually different that they wouldn't apply them in the same way in the same situation.

Chapter 6

Why are ethics flexible and what may cause a change in ethics?

As new information comes into the brain, it adapts to it, it questions it. The result may be that it replaces existing information, it sits alongside that pre-existing information or it is dismissed. The establishment of ethics is no different except that it occurs in an area of the brain that takes longer to develop and mature, and ethics, although a driver of action is not a function that has to occur. Just as there is neuroplasticity in the brain, there is plasticity in ethics. Using ethics is not some instinctive response. It is a considered one. We are not hardwired to use them and as such they can be bypassed depending on the situation.

People, throughout their lives, have a great deal of influences that help form their understanding of the world, their place in it and how they can respond to it. Everyone has a different background and a different range of experiences that influence their understandings of good and bad, right and wrong and what is moral and immoral. They also develop these understandings at vastly different times and in different ways. A core sense of values is reliant on their interaction with people around them. For some people these values are rigidly adhered to and they react as if these values are intrinsic to their being, almost as if they were located in the heart rate and breathing section of the brain. Some would argue that with such intransigent ethics, that people with these are unable to develop further as any new information that comes in is automatically dismissed almost as if it threatens to destroy what has been established. Perhaps that is where the saying "closed minds" comes from.

The question must also be asked about whether there is such a thing as having no ethics or too flexible a set of ethics. The former is extremely unlikely as some even outside imposed ones will be there. It may seem that none are there if they are not used in actions. It may also be the case that any who says that someone else has none is judging that person subjectively based on their own morals and principles. Ethics are things that are referred to and used when appropriate. As for the appropriate time, that is determined by the person themselves. It is that judgement of how and when a core set of values affects actions that differentiate humans from other species.

People change their sense of what is right and wrong subtly as they go through life. For some people there can be major and sometimes sudden shifts caused by outside influences. Some of the big turning points in people's lives may include:

- The loss of a friend or family member
- Breaking up of a relationship
- A close shave with serious injury or death
- Change of schooling or career
- Moving to a new location
- Physical or mental health issues
- Exposure to vastly different information

- Puberty
- Education
- Change in financial circumstances
- Meeting different role models
- Either moving towards or away from religion
- Changing friendship groups
- Overcoming or succumbing to depression
- Seeing how other people live,
- A trip overseas,
- Meeting someone new
- Sometimes it could be a simple trigger such as a book, a film, a song

Any of these or a combination of these and other things can make a person either question consciously their place in the world and what is right and wrong, or subconsciously adapt to the outcomes of these events.

Such events can bring forward an ownership of one's own ethics or potentially delay a change to a set of moral principles. Because everyone thinks differently, there is no set timeline for development of these. Society has expectations that seem to be tied to physical development, but the way our brain functions is not necessarily associated to such outward physical changes. Electrical charges zooming through synapses go at their own pace and take their own paths. That is an essential part of our individuality. To rigidly apply a timetable over the function and development of a person's brain so that everyone was the same, would be a fruitless pursuit. Even in the strictest most regimented educational and religious institutions it doesn't work.

Psychologists, teachers and parents have more success when they provide a loose framework of ethics, explain what they are and give time and space for children and young adults to work out what theirs might be. Imposing a set of moral principles in a time when major changes are occurring and independence is being sought such as during adolescence, is asking for trouble. By around the age of seven, basic ones are usually in place and these will form the beginnings of a lifelong refinement to create a set of principles to live by.

All of these may be challenging experiences may make a person stop and reflect seriously about certain important factors that drive their own actions. The change doesn't have to be a conscious one. New information has been gathered and stored and the conflict may take place subconsciously and is only realised when a set of circumstances arises when a value judgement has to be made. Your brain throws up a red flag and asks you to consider perhaps what happened last time or seeks to use the new information to change your response.

Governments and religious groups would have us all conform to one set of ethics, one set of rules and regulations simply because management of people is so much easier. They would rather have no diversity of thought and opinion for the same reason. This is not to say that a society should not have laws that protect citizens, but that reward and punishment that is a consequence of those laws should take into account the diversity of people. What is deemed right and wrong has always changed over time and laws have always needed to be interpreted and made to fit particular circumstances. This is what happens within people too. Their ethics once established will have a core set of elements that remain constant in most cases, but other elements will remain fluid to adapt to changes in themselves and the world around them.

In any group, any relationship, any family, understandings and beliefs will be shared and unless someone is very dominant, there will be some give and take and adaptation taking place. During a person's life they will move in and out of relationships, in and out of social structures. This will cause change inevitably. Whether that change in ethics is at the fringe or of core beliefs, depends on the individual, the group they move from or into, and the circumstances. In cases whether there is absolute rigidity within a social framework, that can lead to rebellion, a loss of dignity and/or meaningless compliance. An individual returns to the mode they had as a child where they had outside imposed ethics placed upon them.

Because a conscious awareness of your own ethics involves very much a higher order of thinking, many people may not be aware of what they have taken on board and adapted or adopted as their code of behaviour until later in their lives, and for some, not all. This adds another complexity when it comes to a conscious change in their own morality. For many people, change may not seem necessary or may be so subtle that they don't observe it. For others, this change can be quite cataclysmic and even cathartic. People have been known to speak of wrestling with their conscience. What they in fact are doing is having their ethics challenged and responding accordingly. They try to justify to themselves whether to stick with what they know is good and bad, or to respond in a different way. Are they sinning if they do something that goes against their moral principles? Religious groups would have it that they are, if those moral principles are in line with the tenets of the religion. But the only person who is really capable of judging is the person him or herself. For he or she are the only ones who could know most of the reasons why.

Going against a society's laws may not be going against a person's own principles. Is it wrong to dispute a person's ethics? If they are different to your own, you may well want to, but for what purpose? If it is to demonstrate your moral superiority, then the person whom you should question about ethics is yourself. If it is to place in front of them what you believe to be true or "the facts", remember that truth is a moral construct in itself and everyone has different truths. Facts throughout history have charged over time as more and more is understood. If you are trying to lead them down the right path then you need to be sure of the direction, their ability to get to the same destination as you and their willingness to follow you. You may cause confusion, conflict and perhaps send them in the opposite direction. No-one has had all the same life experiences as you. No-one thinks exactly you do. Their truths, their understanding of what is right and wrong will invariably be different to yours. At best you can give them a loose framework and let them construct their own set of moral principles that will keep them in good stead for most of what they face in years to come. Better still is to encourage them to question things and let them find the answers. That way they will own the set of ethics they end up with. People may judge you on your own ethics but if these ethics are owned by you, the only person who should question them is yourself. You are the one who has chosen them. You are the only one who can adapt and change them if necessary. Any ethical dilemma that exists is yours and the way that you deal with it will define to yourself just what sort of person you are.

What do you do when you are faced with an ethical dilemma?

An ethical dilemma is a sign of higher order thinking. It is a recognition that you are aware of the rights and wrongs expectations that either society or yourself have put on you. If you can recognise it is you that have imposed the set of ethics, that is a sign of maturity. Therefore, these sorts of moral questionings have a place in the understanding of yourself as an individual. Recognition is but one step. Working out what led you to the situation where such a dilemma occurred can help to guide you towards a path of resolution. A mentor, trusted friend or in come cases, a family member is a good sounding board, but only if that person does not resort to telling you what you must do. If they suggest options and then leave it to you to make the decision, they can be very valuable.

Often a dilemma, especially for young people is the result of peer pressure and a desire not to appear weak in front of others. However more strength in most situations can be shown by saying no to a dare that clashes with your moral principles. The response from others to your declining to do something against your ethics often says more about them than it does about you. That is not often understood by those who are young.

Taking ownership of the problem you face is critical, because that leaves the decision entirely up to you. True, it means the consequences that follow after you make the decision fall directly on you but that too is a sign of maturity. We see so many people in society who blame others for their own mistakes. These people are hardly the role models you need to look up to.

The saying, "act in haste and repent in leisure" is very apt. If you have time to analyse carefully the problem you face and the options available and their ensuing consequences, you need to take that time. Very few instances require an immediate unthinking response, unless they are life and death situations. Taking control of the situation gives you licence to set the time frame. Again, if someone outside wants to impose their timeframe on you, that says more about them than you. If the decision is important enough for you to believe that a clash of principles is involved, it is just as important that you give any decision the time it deserves.

There are of course various levels of ethical dilemmas. Constant compromising on small issues can be a concern, because when it comes to a major issue, your first inclination could be to compromise through habit. A growing build-up of conceding can also undermine the major principles who hold strong to. You don't have to win every battle, but you can't afford to lose too many small ones as when a major one comes along you need to have the moral resolve to take the time to think things through and decide which path to take.

As mentioned earlier, ethics continue to be modified over time as you gain new experiences and an understanding of the world around you. You do not have to hold fast to what you perceived as being right when you were younger, but you do need to know what has shaped the changes you have made to your ethics. That knowledge is extremely powerful as it gives you a greater understanding of the person you are, the way you think and what is important to you. The latter point is something that changes the most as you age. It actually defines your maturity. Children seek acceptance, security and love. As they grow up those things remain constant but where they find them changes a lot. For some people security comes in the form of material possessions. Acceptance may be tied up in job satisfaction, respect from others and progress through promotion. Friends, partners, children, parents etc may be the source of love in different amounts at different times.

Ethics are formed by interactions. We need to be in situations where there is a two-way flow of ideas. There needs to be an acceptance by other people and yourself that each have different morals and principles. No-one will have the perfect set, nor will anyone have ones that exactly match your own. Arguing that yours are superior may stop you from learning more about other people and therefore stop the interaction that has help establish your own principles. At some point you will find yourself in a situation where your own principles don't give you an answer, however, having an understanding of other people's journey to develop their own set of ethics may assist you in those times.

In short when faced with an ethical dilemma:

- Mentally recognise it and acknowledge it

- Take control of the timeframe for decision making if possible. Do not be bullied by someone else's need for an instant response.

- Work out what has led you to this situation. Was it peer pressure?

- Be aware of your own thinking processes and whether you are prone to compromising and conceding

- Decide on which principles it affects and what ones are non-negotiable

- Come up with a range of options and look at the consequences for these

- Make a decision. Remember, to do nothing is also a decision and may be the right one for you.

- Accept responsibility for whatever action you take

- Reflect and acknowledge that you have done some higher order thinking and that there was learning to be gained that will stand you in good stead in the future, because this won't be the only ethical dilemma that you will face.

How do our beliefs form?

The human brain is an awesome piece of machinery, but it does have its limitations. It can't possibly know everything and respond to everything around it. To make it function effectively in the increasingly complex world we live in, it compartmentalises inputs. It creates stereotypes and makes generalisations. To do otherwise, it would become overwhelmed.

The world's human population is approximately 8.2 billion. There is no way that a human brain can know, let alone rationalise all the individual traits of each person. We therefore pigeonhole people according to categories that we see and have prior knowledge of. That prior knowledge is often what we have been told, but not experienced. Most of the time we first judge on the way people look. Then one of the first organisational aspects is gender. Aligned with that is our expectations of what a male or female is supposed to be, supposed to act, speak, look, behave and think like. These can tell us more about our pre-conceived attitudes than about the other person.

This same initial analysis of another person applies to their ethnicity, their cultural background, their religion, their occupation and possibly even to the football team they follow. As long as we recognise that our brain is doing this basic sorting and that stereotyping does not fully and nor accurately describe an individual, we can move on to find out more about a person and what makes them tick. If we don't move beyond that first level of sorting, we can miss opportunities to learn more about someone else and about ourselves. The complexity of what makes a person who they are at a certain point of time is enormous. Everyone has a back story. Their genetic make-up and their interactions along the way influence who they are.

There are people who use this stereotyping to create fear in others. They paint people as clones. They label them and attribute characteristics to those labels. They even try to confuse us with those labels. An example of that is what is happening in Gaza. Not all Palestinians are Hamas. Not all Jews are Zionists. That confusion is a means to someone else's end. It has led to deliberate death and destruction and attribution of blame.

Anti-Semitism, Islamophobia, misogyny, transphobia, ageism are examples of how people generalise the make-up of others and expect them to conform to our own preconceptions. For many of us our brain's capacity is underutilised. It is being trained to just use basic algorithms to pigeonhole people according to moral and ethical standards that have become ingrained and inflexible. We use prior, sometimes poorly reasoned knowledge, rather than attempting to find out more about someone else. That person's skin may be darker, their religion different, their gender not conforming to norms, and their body shape not matching what is seen in magazines. They may be disabled, have a different socio-economic background and speak a different language, but because they are like that, does that mean they have less rights than we have?

People are not exact clones of each other. Before you criticise someone else, perhaps you should recognise your own individuality, examine it, and celebrate it. Then acknowledge that others have the right to do likewise

Over time we develop a moral and ethical framework to help us make sense of the world around us. Contrary to the belief of some we are not born with it. It is something built up over time. A child, when newborn, has certain reflexive actions to ensure survival. Things such as breathing and crying when in pain, when hungry etc. are not learnt responses. They are inbuilt. They take a great deal of mental application and practice to be able to be controlled. Older children and adults can learn to manipulate their breathing patterns and manage their pain thresholds But, expectations that a baby can master the control of these are unrealistic.

The framework of values is slowly built up from experience and observation. What we are told and learn as a child form the basis of what for many becomes a lifelong code that they live by. It is the reason why children are seen as the most susceptible to outside influence. They have limited experience and knowledge and thus can be influenced far more readily. Although this framework can be seen to be similar for groups of people, because they are based on observation and experience, everyone's moral and ethical standards will have slight variations. Societies tend to homogenise them and attempt to force one particular framework on everyone. The least flexible, the more there is a chance of rebellion. Uniformity caused by outside pressure to conform, stifles individuality.

When we seek to question ideas, we are bombarded with facts. Often these facts are not able to be substantiated, have been carefully selected, placed out of context or even anecdotal. With the surfeit of information being bounced around online it is difficult to gauge the veracity of most of it, because there is usually contradictory data available. Safety lies in echo chambers. We hear the same messages repeated and assume they must be right. At that point, challenging rather than defending them is counter-productive. This is nothing new. Social media is just a faster, broader way of spreading all sorts of 'truths'. Whether we choose to simply agree, ignore, be non-committal about or disagree with them becomes a personal choice. As it was in the past, humans opt for the path of least resistance. It makes life more tolerable. However, being aware that choices are available is an important factor when it comes down to the ownership of your own opinion.

The ability and desire to listen to contradictory views is essential in society. Whether the listener takes on board those ideas, modifies their own or stays affixed to their own is a matter for the individual. If those ideas however cause harm or danger to the individual or others, then society has a right and moral duty to intervene. Cultism, predatory behaviour, and exploitation are examples of when intervention is required, especially when children and people with low cognitive capacity are concerned.

Parroting the words and ideas of another without taking them rationally on board yourself doesn't need a higher level of thinking. In life we accept many things as gospel truth because of who said them, without even questioning what the reasoning was behind such proclamations. It is an impossibility to separately analyse each point raised, determine its origin, its veracity and how it fits into our own ethical and moral framework. To do so would eat heavily into the time available before decisions need to be made or something else demands our attention. Our brain quickly accepts or rejects the information. If accepted, it decides whether action needs to happen straight away, there is time to consider it more fully later, or it should be just filed away with lots of other things and buried deep in our memory until it needs to be recalled. In most situations we aren't aware of the process involved, because it happens in nanoseconds or perhaps, we have been blind-sided and taken unawares.

We make numerous decisions every day that refer back to our preconceived view of the world. Some lead to subtle actions such as a brief nod of approval to someone who fits into our idea of what good behaviour entails. Some lead to less subtle responses including outright hostility towards someone who doesn't. Those still forming their own set of morality and ethics, observe our responses and may use our credibility or lack of it to modify their own framework. In a society nothing is done in isolation. Subliminal impacts on our own accepted understandings occur all the time. These can be found in the things we see on our screens, what we read and what we listen to. In our fast-paced world, we rarely have time to consider what these subliminal ideas are and to question their accuracy and authenticity. What we choose to expose ourselves to may determine our view of the world, but at least we are choosing. There are so many ideas that subtly permeate our minds that we are unaware of. This is even more apparent for children. Advertisers know this. Religions use it. Governments rely on it.

It is the outliers who stand out. They are outliers because of who they are or because they choose to be different. Being so far from the accepted norm, they are often the most creative, but also can be the most dangerous. Some enjoy the notoriety; others bemoan their lack of acceptance. Those closer to the norm may envy the freedom of the outliers, or at alternatively may be revolted by them and denigrate them. We have a moral and ethical continuum, rather than a one size fits all. People move to different points on that continuum at various stages of their lives, as new information comes in, and depending on the situation or aspect. Acknowledging that attitudes change within themselves, but especially within others is difficult for some. People may take pride in the idea that their viewpoint hasn't changed over time. However, it may also signal an unwillingness to take on board new ideas and information, or a belief that their own framework is perfect.

Not only are the set of beliefs that people have on a broad spectrum, but also their understanding and use of them are too. There are people who use them internally and rarely voice them, believing that they are personal. There are others who desire to convert others to their own beliefs, criticise others' beliefs and demand that they be changed. Some people are totally unaware that they have a framework that their brain draws upon, reflect on and drive action.

Self-awareness and understanding of how moral and ethical values are derived does not necessarily correlate with positive attitudes to one's self or to others. It all depends on what is in their framework, to what purpose they use their understanding, and the method of use and impact that it has on others.

Flexibility to modify one's set of beliefs varies too. It depends on one's personal attributes, how ingrained those beliefs are, and the reasons for the change. Those reasons could involve outside pressure to conform, a rational review of them, or even a major life changing event. Many people are so time poor that moments of self-reflection are hard to find. Some are unaware of how their behaviour has been shaped over the years, and may not have the tools, nor see the need to change.

All these situations place people at different places on a range of spectra. There is no ideal, for any ideal is a subjective judgement. People are who they are. Everyone rationalises things differently. Their views on religion, other people's place in society and even the best structure for society will vary greatly. The same applies to so many other things from the everyday mundane ones to personal philosophy. People have all come from different starting points, been influenced by different people, differing amounts of, access to and types of knowledge. They have formed their own truths. They all have different capacities to change their beliefs. Some will be completely intransigent when it comes to changing those truths, while others will go with the flow.

An awareness of how your mind works, what has shaped your belief system and how others think does not make you necessarily a better person, nor smarter or even make better decisions than others. It is just a different trait that you may have amongst other different traits that make you an individual. It can be a curse at times and a blessing at others. It has allowed personal enlightenment for some, and in others, the capacity to manipulate people.

Our mind is a complex entity. Everyone uses theirs differently in different situations. We stereotype. We make generalisations. We use past knowledge and experience to deal with new things we are confronted with. We do this at different speeds, for different reasons and at different levels of thought processing. We have to or we wouldn't be able to cope with all the inputs we receive. Having some sort of moral and ethical framework allows us to rationalise things. It is that framework that often determines our actions, our thoughts, and how we interact with people. Knowing how we developed that framework, and the content and context of it may give us greater insight into our own attitudes and behaviours.

MAKING A DIFFERENCE

The truth is that very few of us end up in a position where we can make a real difference, yet, that is what we have been conditioned to believe that we have the opportunity to do, must strive to do, or find an avenue to be able to do. The danger in such conditioning is that people can be made to feel that doing anything less is regarded as a failure.

Parents urge their children to find careers that either make a difference and/or make money. Teachers subconsciously push students in the same direction, and society only celebrates the few who actually do make a difference, not those who tried and failed or those who had no chance.

It depends on the definition of making a difference though. Simply by being born, people are making a difference, each person has an impact on society. It is just the size of the impact differs. The interactions that humans have with each other and the world around them has a causality effect that influences future events and other people's actions thereafter.

The saying that "If a tree falls in the forest and no-one hears it, does it make a sound"? can be interpreted as questioning whether that tree really existed. That tree will have had an impact on the world around it when it was standing. It will continue having an impact as it rots and decays. Some falling trees have bigger impacts. Why should humans believe they are different?

Some say that we are pre-programmed to aspire to do better, and therefore we set high and often unachievable goals. Failing to reach those goals is seen as a personal failure and with that comes the negative feelings such as the feeling of inadequacy. What if the goals were wrong?

Young children are asked what they want to be when they grow up and are praised when they say things such as doctors, police officers, teachers or nurses. What would our reaction be if a child said things like, happy, content, or even, loved? Perhaps we are not giving children the scope to think beyond a career path as an answer. More often than not the career they nominate as a child will not be the one they pursue or have the opportunity to pursue when they become adults. To be happy, content and feel loved are more worthy goals and possibly more achievable goals that they can hold firm to all their lives.

As a friend pointed out, perhaps the question of children, if not all of us, is not what do you want to be, but who do you want to be?

STARING BLINDLY INTO THE ABYSS

A political essay

By Greg Tuck

CONTENTS

INTRODUCTION

There is a perception among the public that the way the current governmental system operates is ponderously slow, archaic and dominated by people who seem to be playing political power games and not for what they were elected to do. From the outcomes being achieved, the public perception appears to be correct. It appears that politicians live in their own private world enshrouded in a bubble of lack of awareness of what everyday Australian life is really like. Frustrated by that inability to get through to their elected representatives and enduring what is at times blatant insensitivity, voters have become disenchanted and are turning away from showing any interest in what are important decisions that are being made that affect their lives. To a certain extent it could be said that disillusionment and disinterest plays into the hands of some politicians who are unwilling to listen to, heed the advice of, and act in accordance with, the opinions of the people they represent. So where has it all gone wrong? Indeed, has it *all* gone wrong? Let's look at the various mechanisms that exist in the structure of our government, how they were initially designed to operate and how they actually operate. But first, in summation the following are the shortfalls of our system that are seen by a lot of the public

Australia's government system appears to be failing in many ways.

It fails to:

- properly engage voters,

- achieve outcomes,

- react to changed conditions quickly,

- be accountable to the public,

- use taxpayer money judiciously,

- plan for the future beyond the next election cycle

- see beyond political gamesmanship

- use its time efficiently

- be transparent

- communicate the reasons why decisions were made

- present an outlook that has moved into the 21st century

- be aware of how the community actually lives and make decisions accordingly

Questions arise therefore as to the cause. Is it

1. The restrictive structure of the Australian Constitution?
2. The type of Westminster organisation of parliament itself?
3. The adversarial system in place that is not being used appropriately to achieve best outcomes.
4. The party systems that have flourished?
5. The types of people who are elected?

THE CONSTITUTION

125 years ago, a new nation was about to be born. At its core was to be a constitution

The process began with the National Australasian Convention in 1891, followed by further conventions in the mid-1890s. Australia at the time was a series of British colonies that had formalised into six self-governing states. There were no territories as such when Australia became officially a nation in 1900 with the passing of a bill in the British Parliament. Australia had outgrown the notion of merely being a British colony. The discovery of gold in the 1850s, the emergence of the industrial revolution and the increased wealth that these, farming and mining brought allowed Australia to be more than just a colonial extension of England. A majority of people in Australia in the 1890s were actually born in Australia. The time was ripe for nationhood.

A group of men from each state met to frame a new constitution. There were no women as the society was still very patriarchal despite the suffrage movement.

The constitution was constructed in such a way that two houses were designed to have a Washminster system. It would have functions like the Westminster system of Britain, but with no House of Lords. Instead, the second house, as with the Washington model, would have a senate representing the states.

The constitution was for a federation of states. Electorates based on population numbers would have representation in the lower house (The House of Representatives). Because it was a federation, six representatives from each state would form the senate. Their task was to review legislation and ensure that the states were not disadvantaged by the legislation, or that one state achieved much better outcomes than others.

The Commonwealth Electoral Act 1902 set up the framework for the Commonwealth electoral system, which was administered until 1916 as a branch of the Department of Home Affairs, by the Department of Home and Territories until 1928, back to Department of Home Affairs to 1932, and then Department of the Interior until 1972. The Australian Electoral Office was finally created in 1973 by the Australian Electoral Office Act 1973 and became an independent body.

The voting for the state representatives in the senate was made complex in 1948 as there was a change in first past the post voting. This was in acknowledgement that senators were often not independent representatives of their states but in fact represented their party. After 1948, there was to be a quota system involved where a certain percentage of a statewide vote determined who was elected. Initially there were six senators in each state in the parliament, but that number that has since grown to twelve. A senator is elected when a quota is achieved. Any votes in excess of the quota are distributed in the preferential order of the electors. It became even more complicated with senators serving for a period of six years rather than three as in the House of Representatives. Half of the senate would be elected at an election for the House of Representatives, unless the government called a double dissolution which would mean all senators regardless of term length served would face an election. The six-year terms and half rotation was supposed to allow for continuity of the senate process of review.

In 1911 South Australia ceded the North part of its state (Northern Territory) to federal government to allow it become a territory. For a long period of time the territory had no representation in the Senate. The Northern Territory finally gained Senate representation in 1975. This occurred after the passage of the Senate (Representation of Territories) Act 1973, which allowed both the Northern Territory and the Australian Capital Territory to elect two senators each. The first senators for the territories were elected in December of that year.

Voting for the House and the Senate was based on the notion of one person, one vote. Voting would be done in secret ballots first introduced to the world in Australia. People would be able to have their voice heard in parliament. It would be put forward by local and state representatives. In return they would be notified why decisions were made. That was the theory. As in life, theory and practice can be two different animals.

Areas were ceded by the states such as powers for national defence, trade and treaties. These now came under the control of the new federal government. If any of the states had disagreements with how these were being handled, or thought their state was being unfairly treated, they had representatives in the Senate who could call for changes to be made.

A number of amendments over the years have been proposed but only eight have been successful.

- In 1906 the amendment allowed for Senators' terms to commence in July instead of January. (The idea was to have senate and house elections to be held simultaneously.)

- In 1910 the amendment allowed the Commonwealth to take over state debts. (This was important so that Australia worked economically as one nation not a mix of different states with different economic rules)

- In 1928 the amendment allowed for the financial agreements between the Commonwealth and states regarding public debts. (This was timely as Australia still owed Britain money to cover expenses incurred during World War 1. It was ironic in a way that Australia came to the aid of Britain and Britain charged Australia for the privilege. It was also timely as the Great Depression hit the world a year later.)

- In 1946 the amendment allowed the Commonwealth power to legislate on a range of social services. (Following the Second World War, an Australia-wide social safety net needed to be introduced to support those most in need.

Rationing was still in place until 1950 when Australia's economic "long boom" began.)

- In 1967 the amendment allowed the removal of discriminatory references to Aboriginal people in the Constitution and allowed the Commonwealth to make laws for them. (Aboriginal people had been given the right to vote in federal elections in 1962. The constitutional amendment in 1967 was about the need to remove discrimination across Australia in many areas.)

- In 1977 the amendment allowed casual vacancies in the Senate are filled by a person of the same political party as the previous senator. (This came after the dismissal of the Whitlam government in 1975 and highlighted the power of parties in politics. It took away the right of states to nominate anyone to fill a casual vacancy. Ostensibly this was to stop states with different political allegiances from stacking the senate. However, it has caused many controversial appointments and allowed non-voter elected people to make decisions in the senate.)

- In1977 this amendment allowed electors in the territories to vote in referendums. (This had seemed obvious and should have been in place as soon as territories were set up, but the strange way that success in referendums is determined made it very complicated because territories were not states.)

- In 1977 this amendment set a retiring age of 70 for High Court and federal court judges. (This was to bring the federal system in line with the states. It was also a recognition that some judges may not be capable of making rational decisions after the age of 70, and removing them from that position was an extremely awkward proposition.)

There is an inherent difficulty in getting any constitutional amendment to be passed. It is the "double majority" requirement. This double majority is achieved when more than half of the voters from all around Australia vote YES. and a majority of voters in at least 4 states vote YES.

Our voting system is not part of the constitution per se and is handled by federal government legislation which is then administered but an independent impartial body currently known as the Australian Electoral Commission (AEC). However, because voting determines the constitution via the referendum process some background is included here.

Initially only men over the age of 21 could vote, but not all of them. Indigenous men were not given permission to vote. Changes to electoral laws were made separate to the constitution to remedy the situation over time.

- In 1902, women aged 21 and over were given the right to vote and stand for election in federal elections.

- In 1962, the right to vote was finally extended to all Aboriginal and Torres Strait Islander peoples, including women, in federal elections.

- In 1973 18-year-olds were allowed to vote. This followed an extensive campaign pointing out that these same people were deemed responsible to be able drink, to drive, and be sent off to war but not allowed to vote to not be sent off to that war.

- Compulsory voting was also introduced in 1924. Theoretically this guaranteed that everyone had a say.

The constitution is essentially a framework. The fact that it has had few changes to it may be because:

- It isn't too definitive.

- It was well framed in the first place.

- It is difficult to change.

- There is a general lack of understanding in the population about how politics and in particular the constitution works.

- Any proposed changes are weaponised by political parties.

The constitution enshrines the separation of powers – the judiciary, the government, the head of state, the public service and the defence force. Whilst these interact, each has its own separate role, independence and function.

Australia's constitution also ensures the differentiation between the three levels of government: Federal, State (or Territory), and Local.

Each level has its own powers, responsibilities, and services, and they are all elected by the people they govern.

The Constitution does not outline the powers of ministers and the prime minister. Instead, it vests executive power in the Governor-General who then passes those powers by convention on to the parliament which has operated under the Westminster system.

WESTMINSTER ORGANISATION OF PARLIAMENT

The Westminster system is a hangover from British governments over the years. With some modifications it has remained relatively intact and is supposed to encourage accountability to the public for a government's actions and agenda. Once parliamentarians are elected in Australia's case, the prime minister is elected from the floor of the House of Representatives. That person must have to be able to hold the majority of votes and is subject to a no confidence motion should that support ever waver. In that case, a vote can be called on the floor and a new replacement be sought. The alternative is for the prime minister to seek the Governor General's consent to have another election. It is possible to run with what is called a hung parliament whereby just enough votes are received but only for the guarantee of supply, I.e. the passage of bills to allow government departments to run.

Ministers are more often than not selected by the Prine Minister and they form a cabinet which functions as an executive where decisions are made. These decisions can be acted upon if they are changes to regulations, but if legislation is required, then bills go before parliament. Ministers must come from either the Senate or the House of Representatives. That way there is more accountability as these people are elected and face an election which allows the public to assess and vote on the capacity to do the job. This is unlike what happens in the US where a president is elected and he/she chooses people to head departments. These people are only accountable to the President.

As part of the accountability process, an opposition is set up which also comes from the floor of either chamber. The actual purpose is to scrutinise work in departments and of ministers and stimulate debate over contentious issues, in order to refine legislation. Committees are also set up to examine in fine detail proposals and outcomes. The Westminster system has a number of checks and balances. There are areas that do overlap between the judiciary, executive, parliament and public service, because they must work together. A couple of examples are when a piece of legislation may be in breach of the constitution it is up to the High Court to rule on such matters. Nominations to be on the High Court are in the hands of the Attorney General. There is also the fact that various heads of the public service and judiciary are appointed by the parliament/executive and this leaves the process open to political manipulation. The appointment of ambassadors is one example in particular where political interference has come to light because a basic political message needs to be passed on between countries and a government uses past politicians to pass on messages that toe "the company line."

The Governor General is often a political appointment as well and is effectively the head of state, although that has become a more ceremonial position in the main. Only in 1975 has the Governor General ever intervened to dismiss a government. It was within John

Kerr's powers at the time, but many saw that as an abuse of power and a blatant act of political interference.

Under the Westminster system, votes on legislation are taken on the floor of either house. The legislation and any added amendments must pass both houses to become law. All bills passed are nominally signed off by the Governor General.

There is a lot of ceremony attached to the Westminster system. The various rites and the formality are often outdated and mean that sticking to past rules can make the passing of legislation slow, tedious and suffer long unnecessary delays. There are flaws in the Westminster system mainly due to the fact that it hasn't adapted over time and is able to be easily manipulated.

As previously mentioned, the Westminster system was introduced to assist the operation of parliament. It was to assist in the informed debating of legislation and to allow greater scrutiny of ministerial directions. The Westminster system has suffered at the hands of party politics and bears little resemblance to what it could and should be.

THE ADVERSARIAL SYSTEM

The idea of adversarial debate has merits. It means that decisions are talked through, opinions sought and that those voting on legislation have a better understanding of its importance, ramifications and consequences which may have initially been unintended. Parliament is meant to be a contest of ideas where such things are discussed at length, compromises are sought to secure the best legislation possible. A government that sticks by the principles of such debate and produces the best-informed legislation by discussion, compromise and consensus is hardly autocratic or dictatorial.

This presupposes that everyone can have their own personal viewpoint and is free to speak on that in Parliament. By having diverse opinions expressed by a broad range of people within a community, there is a stronger likelihood that legislation will suit a broad range of people. That sort of debate should happen on the floor of each chamber so that transparency of decision making is available to the public.

One of the many problems that may arise is that people may not get the opportunity to speak and thus their electorate's voice is not heard. This can be caused by the nature of the person elected, time constraints and political use of the unspoken rules of parliament. Another drawback us that adversarial politics often invites the notion that there are only two solutions to a problem. There may be a variety of them, but people may be forced to take sides and choose between just two and not even have the opportunity to put forward an alternative. At the end of debate, there will be winners and losers. People may see legislation as either right or wrong. There is a risk that working together to get the best outcome will be lost in the way that the process is used these days. This comes down to how debate is managed by participants, the arbiters (president of Senate, speaker of the House of Representatives) should be independent but invariably are not.

The adversarial notion of debate that has designed to improve things has taken a different form. Two groups argue simplistically that one is right and the other is wrong. There are only winners and losers and few people seem capable of working together to achieve the best possible outcomes for the public. It has become a game, a bad piece of theatre that many people in the community turn away from.

With Australian politics has descended into an us versus them approach where two adversaries are pitted against each other, only one is in power and the other spends its time working out how to get into power. Voters elect people to get specific jobs done and little gets done of long-lasting value because of the infighting, back biting and backstabbing that takes place in parties and between parties. There may be a better way of doing things.

POLITICAL PARTIES

Even before nationhood, political parties dominated the scene at a state level. It was a common practice in most democratic countries. People of like minds would join together, discuss issues and form a consensus of opinions on various political aspects. Many of these were formalised and rules were formed about who could be a member of a political party and how that political party would function. In effect, this meant that teams of people would go into a parliamentary debate with fixed opinions determined behind closed doors at party room meetings.

Reasons for those decisions did not have to be made public and only a vote on the floor of one of the chambers was required. Transparency and consultation with a politician's electorate were not seen of great importance. The party room determined the policy. The original policy was often determined prior to a party room meeting by unelected people at party conventions or by behind-the-scenes operatives. Some people saw this as circumventing the democratic process of parliament itself. Others thought that it was beneficial as it saved time and long-winded debate in the chamber. However, with decisions being made by people who weren't accountable to the public, powerful and influential non-elected members of society had a lot of say in what went on.

There were a number of small parties in the initial federal parliament but gradually two rose to the fore especially after the second world war. One was based on labour and workers and the other on business, mining and farmers. One was a single party, the other a coalition of two parties. Similar to the parties in British politics, one was progressive and the other conservative.

It was not until 1977 the political parties were actually acknowledged in the constitution. They were not part of the constitution and not really until 1910 were they a factor in parliament. Since that point in time, at a federal level, dominant parties have consisted of Labor, and a range of conservative parties that have merged and been in Coalition. Currently we have Labor, and a coalition of Liberal and National parties. The remaining members of parliament are independent or in very small parties. Those in major parties tend to represent their party rather than their electorate. This has spread into the Senate where senators seem nominally tagged to a state but serve their party first and foremost. Party rules are strictly enforced to the point where people cannot independently speak on the floor of either chamber. They may air their grievances in closed party room meetings but may face disendorsement at the next election if they exercise their right to express a contrary opinion to their party as an MP or senator in parliament, even if that opinion best reflects their electorates views.

From the public's perspective, political parties are seen as a good thing as the range of policies put forward at election time by large parties makes it easier for people to choose between candidates standing in electorates. However, they may know what they are voting for but know little about who they are voting for. People are being encouraged to vote for a brand and, if the truth be known, for a party colour in some cases. What is put forward by political parties at the time of election does not bind them to actually implementing them. In some cases, there have been policies put forward merely to differentiate parties between themselves. Small parties or a large party that knows it won't win at an election can and often do, offer policies that can't and never will be implemented.

The concept of people meeting together to discuss issues and future legislation appears laudable. It is important to remember the value of people talking about political matters with others who are like-minded. Where the current political party system is failing at present is due to the rigidity of the party system. On contentious matters people are expected to vote along party lines. Any divergence from that can see members excommunicated from the party even if abstaining or voting against a party directive is in the best interests of the electorate that the person represents. Issues may be raised in the party room and these are dealt with behind closed doors and out of the public view. Members are expected to agree with the decision made behind those doors and not discuss issues outside. Transparency of process is not encouraged. It appears that party unity is more important than a person's electorate. Where it also fails is that if one party raises a workable piece of legislation, it must be opposed by those on the other side of the chamber. No wonder the public is disenchanted and sees the process of debate as a farce, and little more than juvenile school yard antics. Politicians are seen as attention seeking, insincere people who deliberately stand in the way of improving things in a range of areas. Indeed, some politicians see the whole process as some sort of game where the aim is to get themselves into power at almost any cost. If that means lying, spreading misinformation and disinformation, and even making personal attacks on colleagues, then so be it. Indeed, these are strategies that parties use against each other. The benefits of having parties are lost because how the party system operates. Any credibility of the party process fades away when it means that a parliamentarian has to choose between what their electorate wants and what their party wants, and choose their party, then there is something wrong. There is also something wrong when people can't speak freely on the floor of either chamber of parliament. It is the machinations, power plays, political intrigue, manipulation of party members, playing of political games, behind-the-scenes unelected string pullers and strict party rules that make political parties appear more like a blight on democracy than a tool to make it function better.

CANDIDATES AND PARLIAMENTARIANS

It is preferable if we get a wide range of people with different skills and life experiences in parliament. People from different types of communities and different socio-economic backgrounds can give a more well-rounded knowledge base for decision making. Given the large size of electorates, particularly in the senate, it is impossible to expect that each parliamentarian can effectively consult with their constituents. Indeed, some parliamentarians use that as an excuse for consulting very little. Diversity is important, but people also need the ability to speak up for their communities. Often that doesn't happen because opportunities aren't made available in parliament, party rules don't permit it, or intimidation takes place. Therefore, it becomes even more important that the Speaker of the House of Representatives and the President of the Senate keep an independent tight rein on proceedings. Too often parliaments are dominated by people who like hearing the sounds of their own voices, wander off on tangents, use the forum for party politicking or personal put downs. This has been happening since federation, but has become more prevalent and noticeable of late.

Lawyers and barristers, managers and consultants make up about one in five MPs in the federal Labor, Greens, National and Liberal parties. Former political staffers make up over 40% of Labor MPs, over 30% for the Liberal party and 20% for the Nationals. This path to power narrows the representation of communities. While it may seem preferable to have lawyers as politicians as they are making laws, there is an effective public service that can turn policies into legislation.

By narrowing the scope of people being pre-selected by parties, people with expertise in other areas miss out on the opportunity. Given also the rigmarole and the toxic workspace, many talented people choose not to enter politics. Pre-selection for political parties is not conducive to diversity. Various expectations are put forward by the small number of people who actually decide on pre-selections. This lack of diversity extends even to this day. One example is in the form of beliefs that 50% of the population has to jump higher hurdles to be considered by some parties, particularly for winnable seats. In 1902 women were first given the right to vote. They were also able to stand for seats in parliament from 1902 onwards. However, it was not until 1943 that Dame Enid Lyons was elected to the House of Representatives for the seat of Darwin in Tasmania, and Dame Dorothy Tangney was elected to the Senate representing the state of South Australia. Since then, it has been a very slow process to increase the number of women in parliament as they were often preselected in unwinnable seats. Labor put in quotas in 1994 to address the issue. The Coalition, particularly the Liberals, do not believe in quotas and merely say that all pre-selection is done on merit. It is hard to believe in this day and age that so few women are found by Liberal pre-selection panels to have as much merit as men.

As mentioned before a candidate in a winnable seat is actually chosen by a very small number of people. They meet, submit their preferred candidates to a state review panel that occasionally overrides that decision and parachutes someone else in. In the case of the Liberal party, unspoken bonus points appear to be awarded:

- If you are a male,

- If you have been part of the IPA,

- If you have the backing of significant donors

- If have a certain smug, born to rule attitude.

If you don't meet those four key selection criteria, then you are seen to be in danger of eventually becoming a Teal. The Liberals seem unable to know what to do with intelligent assertive women, who according to their ideology should be at home looking after the children, or attending charitable events, and feeling comfortable playing second fiddle as a Stepford wife. Most Liberal pre-selection panels are made up of stalwarts of the party. Given that very few young people are joining political parties, the stalwarts are usually fifty or older. For the older Liberal women on pre-selection panels who decide on who the candidate will be, it appears only males are suitable as candidates. This is probably due to very dated and conservative attitudes about the roles of women. For the ageing males on the pre-selection panel, women with intellect can be seen as a threat because these males might be shown up as less than competent by comparison. It means that mediocrity becomes embedded and celebrated.

So, what can women do beyond imbibing testosterone and having radical surgery? They could gather together and reshape the Liberal party by moving it beyond the 1950s, or join the growing number of independents who don't see any of the major parties as a viable option because of political ideology in one and sexism and misogyny in the other. However, as some women have done in the past, they could act the dumb blond, take the arm of a rising Liberal male who is even dumber, but can be controlled behind the scenes. Until there is a significant change in the minds of those preselectors or even just in who decides pre-selections, the diversity needed in parliament by the Liberal party will remain missing.

To be a member of parliament, you need to be an Australian citizen. Indigenous people were granted citizenship in 1948 but weren't able to vote until 1962. Neville Bonner was the first person of indigenous descent elected to federal parliament in the senate in 1971. The first Asian-Australian member of Parliament was Tsebin Tchen who entered the Senate in 1999. Citizenship for non-Europeans was not granted until 1957 but you had to be a resident for fifteen years. This was later reduced to three years in 1973. The first Muslim elected was Ed Husic in 2010.

Australia has not handled diversity at all well when it comes to citizenship, voting rights and election of non-European people over the years. Our parliament probably has missed out on so much valuable experience, advice and skills that were on offer. It continues today where the vast majority of people in parliament are white, over the age of 50 and of European descent. There is currently parity between genders but back in 2002 the split was 74% male 26% female. Much of the gender change has happened in the minor parties, independents and in Labor. Currently, out of two hundred and twenty-six senators and MPs, Australia has only twenty non-European parliamentarians, including eight Indigenous MPs and senators. This is despite only around thirty percent of women in the Coalition. 77 % of politicians have a bachelor's degree or higher which may be handy but far exceeds the average of 32% across the nation. There appears to be an over representation of highly educated people and this may mean that they may not understand what normal people go through.

What we are finding one and a quarter centuries after Federation is that many people who are attracted to enter and stay in politics are the unexceptional and the power hungry. That is not healthy for proper democratic debate, decision making and ensuring legislation is not benefitting one sector of society over another.

INTERIM SUMMARY

In summation:

The constitution holds up pretty well. It is only a framework.

The Westminster system, if it is properly applied has merit, although much more can be achieved by people working together.

Adversarial political debate has many drawbacks. The aim should be to achieve some workable consensus and not have a divisive outcome.

Political parties, who have set positions created behind closed doors on proposed legislation destroy transparency and accountability. Their rules inhibit freedom of speech and delay legislation often for the flimsiest reason so that their party's agenda, which is often formulated by outsiders, can be pushed forward. Over time, the parties need to change to become more relevant, more representative, or they need to disappear entirely. The change in culture that would flow from this would see far better:

- More representative candidates would stand for election. And these people would hopefully have wisdom, foresight, capacity to compromise and a genuine selflessness.
- Civilised real debating would occur by people who are there for the right reasons. Time would not be wasted on party politics

- Important legislation would be created, debated and passed (or amended as required) so that it isn't out of date before it is enacted.

The people whom we elect to serve are actually doing us a disservice. Many are more interested in power games and what they can gain out of their position, be it notoriety, monetary gains or status.

<u>**IMMEDIATE CHANGES**</u>
Things that could immediately change are:

- Sending things to committees. Currently that is seen as a way of delaying or defeating legislation before it gets voted on. The time lag between tabling proposed legislation, voting on it and implementing it is disgraceful and if government were a business, it would not survive. There is more focus currently being put on playing politics than the core business of being a senator or MP. It would be far better if any MP could propose a piece of legislation and it go to various committees set up to examine specific portfolios. Their job is to expediently liaise with the proponent and then refine the legislation so that it may be voted on in parliament.

- Changing the Speaker/President of the Senate arrangements

- The use of a member of parliament as a speaker or president does not work effectively. The job of the parliamentarians is to read, listen and vote. Currently the speaker/president has a casting vote but can't speak on behalf of their electorate on legislation so to a certain extent that electorate is not represented in parliament. Someone with a high court judge qualification should be brought in to facilitate the debates and have powers to exclude members or senators from the chamber.

- While it is understood that various ministers and the PM may need to be absent from sittings occasionally, all members should attend every sitting. Sittings of parliament need to increase. Currently less than fifty days per year is the norm and they are not full days as Mondays start at noon and Fridays end at noon and Tuesday mornings are set aside for political party meetings. If political parties' meetings are held out of hours as they should be, because they are really only about political strategy rather than legislation refinement, there would be more time able to be devoted to legislation and committee work. It might be better to have one full week devoted to committee work, one week devoted to electoral work and two full weeks devoted to parliamentary sittings. There seems to be an inordinate amount of time spent by politicians not doing what they were elected to do. Accountability in terms of time should be beefed up. It is hard to understand why some politicians traipse all over the country supporting their party and often to the detriment of their electorate. They should get four weeks annual leave from mid-December to mid-January like most employees. Perhaps that should be in their EBA and job description.

LONG-TERM CHANGES

We have a government that functions, but it could function a whole lot better. The following are some long-term changes that might enhance our governance. These are long term as the culture of parliament would need to change and a change in culture takes time.

Step one

Abolish parties as structures. In reality these are really lobby groups who wish to impose their own ideology onto the public. In turn, they are lobbied by other groups or individuals who are seeking benefits for their own personal, association's or company's game. These groups will demand something in return. As such, the chance of corruption is higher and deals are hidden behind political party facades.

There is a lot of parliamentary time taken up with trying to bring down the other side. There would be less money spent and allocated towards promotion of political parties at election time. Currently individuals standing as candidates get monetary support, but political parties get extra, which is an unfair advantage.

Under the current system, electors identify with a party rather than an individual and they might not get the best person to represent them. Party politics at a local level may see a small group of people deciding who their preferred candidate is. That person then gets the weight of the party behind them and, as many of the seats are won on party lines, and it is really only that small group of people who are the ones who have decided on a candidate.

However, there are many things that preclude us having a parliament that is devoid of party politics.

- There is an extensive history of it being in Australia that has been massaged to indicate that this form of government has delivered the best outcomes, without any shortcomings.
- Business, union and other groups believe they must have larger bodies to "negotiate" with. This allows them to push their interests by offering larger donations to a few rather than smaller to a lot, one of whom might call them out for trying to influence an outcome.
- There is a misconception by many that proper debate will be difficult and the that the continuation of scripted adversarial debate must continue.
- Change may see the public less disenchanted and the current actions and outcomes therefore face more scrutiny and higher demands for transparency.
- There is a belief that we must have a Ford vs Holden, us vs them mentality to give freedom of choice. However, this division actually restricts choice as only two options are placed before the public on most occasions.
- The presentation of a common voice and message overrides the concerns of individual electorates and allows parties to do virtually as they please.

- Candidates for elections prefer to hide behind generalisations rather than be identified by who they are and what they actually stand for.

- The people who are in the position of power and thus who can make changes are the ones who will be affected the most. Self-interest will ensure no change.

<u>Step two</u>

Dispense with adversarial form of debate as it isn't working. If everyone elected is there for the right reasons, then working together should achieve consensus or at least a vote on legislation on the floor and not decided by parties behind closed doors. Everyone elected becomes part of the government and there are no designated spots for crossbenchers and opposition. This may mean that there is a furniture rearrangement required in the chambers. Everyone can speak on a piece of legislation and takes equal responsibility for everything voted on, with a simple majority passing legislation. Again, that means electors will see whether their representative is voting accordioning to what they said they would when standing for election.

Currently we have an opposition that appears to be blocking legislation based on trying to embarrass the government. They spend their time scoring points, delaying legislation and preparing for the next election. They are supposed to assist their constituents in a meaningful way. In fact, they come across as unemployed for three years until they get into power. Even the wording of "opposition" is taking literally. If they aren't the ones that come up with ideas, then they oppose it.

If there was no opposition, then there would be no need for a leader of the opposition. That person currently and wrongly is given almost prime ministerial status and a high salary that is not deserved.

Step three

Change the way the senate is elected. Once again, the quota system isn't working. It is decided on party lines and many candidates don't get a look in if they don't belong to a party. This is most evident when people are able to vote above the line. The senate should be made up of people wishing to stand up to represent their state. Currently votes are done on party lines. The notion that a state government and not the people select a replacement from a party should a senator, retire, resign or die in office is not democratic, even if as the constitution requires that replacement senator must come from the same political party. An election for a senate vacancy should be held as soon as possible after the vacancy is known.

Step four

Change preferential voting to first past the post in the House of Representatives as long as a candidate receives over 50% of the vote. If a candidate doesn't get over 50%, then the top two are voted on again. This works well in other countries. In the senate where six seats for states are decided, 16.6% or more should secure a seat. A secondary vote may be needed to decide on seats not allocated. This secondary vote means that there will be more cost involved, but we should get better candidates and not have someone who manages to get in with a low first preference count, but through preference deals.

Step five

- Elections should be held every four years at a set date. A half senate will be voted on every four years, One half with the House of Representatives and the other half with a two-year gap between the House of Representatives.

- Real time expenditure reporting needs to occur when candidates spend on electioneering. Any donations (over $2) must be declared and failure to declare donations could be a cause for a candidate to be dismissed if criminality is proven. Equal election funding should be made available to each candidate. Currently outside sponsorship and extra money being allocated to "parties" means that there is not a level playing field. No-one should be able to buy their way into a seat.

- The Prime Minister is elected from the floor of joint sitting of parliament. That person needs to get over 50% of the vote of parliamentarians. If not the top two get voted on. The same applies for the deputy PM.

- Ministers for various portfolios are nominated and voted on by parliament. They are elected solely on merit and capacity to do the job.

- Any conflict of interest is to be noted for any parliamentarian and they need to abstain from voting on any legislation where that applies. However, should that disqualify over a third of members, then all may vote.

<u>Step 6</u>

Promote the idea that standing for election is not for those who chase glory, status, wealth and power. That selflessness not selfishness is at its core.

In years gone by, perhaps because politicians lacked as much scrutiny as they get now, they were far more respected. The current crop appear to demand respect without necessarily earning it. The expect plaudits for just doing their job without recognising that all the rest of us are just doing our jobs for far less perks and salary. We have had politicians who have improperly used their position and have rorted the system. In any other situation they would have been sacked or even gaoled. They instead have merely had to apologise, pay back what is owed and expected to have learnt their lesson. That lesson is to them to not get caught.

We expect our politicians to be role models and set examples for others. They fall short of that mark even on the floor of the chamber where debating has become a farce and the standard of behaviour is more reminiscent of a school yard.

The whole culture needs to change to attract the best people. Currently the people we elect merely perpetuate and exacerbate the situation. If politicians wish to be respected, they need to respect the lofty office that they have been elected to. They need to understand that it isn't just a game of matching wits, and taking an opposing view. The decisions they make have real consequences, perhaps not for them, but for those in the community, particularly those in need and most at risk.

we need parliamentarians who will listen far more than they speak, who will take on board new ideas, who are independent from party politics and who will have only the best interests of all Australians at heart. There needs to be a sign outside all doors of Parliament House that says *"Get down off your high horses. Park your wheelbarrows outside. Leave your egos in the cloakroom. This is a place of work, not self-worship."*

<u>**CONCLUSION**</u>

Our government system is failing on many fronts, but just because it appears to have always been this way, doesn't mean it has to stay that way in the future. We need the brightest and best minds in the country to run our trillions of dollars economy. We need to have the clearest thinkers who can accurately predict and plan for the future, not just for the three-year parliamentary period, but long term.

Our politicians are staring blindly into the abyss of an uncertain future while desperately clinging to an irrelevant past they helped create and think will save us. To paraphrase a quote wrongly attributed to Albert Einstein,

" The essence of stupidity is doing the same thing over and over and expecting a different result."

We have become so regimented and constrained in our thinking that we believe what may have been suitable a hundred years ago can remain unchanged now. Our political process has not moved with the times and we elect people who feel comfortable playing a game by ancient rules that suit them and not the situation. It is time that we changed what began 125 years ago. What was seen as a workable form of governance back then has morphed into something that is unwieldy, slow and dominated by political games rather than good legislation. We don't need to throw the baby out with the bath water but take the best bits and enhanced those, toss out the parts that aren't working, and look at ways that the rest can be to reconfigured to make a government that puts people first.

Stereotyping in Literature – The Annuals Example

A Discussion Paper

By Greg Tuck

Contents

<u>**Introduction**</u>

The question needs to be asked, did the publishers of books in the late nineteenth century though to the mid twentieth century select literature for the public because it reflected society at the time, or did they try to use their selections to influence and control society? We do not have a time machine to transport us back to that era to see what was taking place. Even if we did have, we still might not have been able to view the true motivations of publishers and others who had a lot of influence over literature. Each person involved in the process has their own special filters to pass the literary efforts of authors through when deciding what will get published and the market that will be supplied. Not all published works were about making profit. Other agendas were at play.

In today's society, we are more acutely aware of propaganda, of echo chambers, of misinformation and disinformation, but the general public of the 1850s through to the mid-1960s took what was written as the gospel truth.

Censorship has always been a factor in literature. It has been used to stifle thought and free speech. In English literature, Chaucer, Shakespeare and Dickens had to weave their political commentary into their poems, plays and stories. Whether this was at the behest of publishers is not known, or perhaps it was necessary so as not to offend powerful people.

The publishers of books had enormous amount of control of the thinking of everyday people. In the early years before and just after the first printing press was made, religious denominations made the most of the technology available and the population most of whom were illiterate were led to believe that books held in their pages the meaning of life.

The control of the printed word became the domain of publishers and governments rather than the churches from the middle to the end of the industrial revolution through to today, although the medium today has changed.

The reason for the change was that once the industrial revolution began, it became more and more obvious that a better educated population was required to continue the progress and manage the new technologies. Ignorant peasant farm workers had to be upskilled to manage new machinery. Schools for all became more commonplace and in various states within Australia, compulsory education became the norm.

A greater quantity of reading material was required beyond the scientific, religious and philosophical writings of the past. People, including those on factory floors, needed to have a certain amount of education so that they could do the work required of them. Education became valued and provided social mobility. In the main it was based on written language. Publishing of material expanded as did the different genres of writing. Publishers were at the centre of this educational revolution. But did their books, the stories and poems they selected to print, reflect the life at the time or a life that people were supposed to aspire to. What was behind the selection of material? Were they providing the public with what the public wanted, or were they trying to influence the political, moral, and social values of the people who would read the books?

As major events occurred, fashion changed, political situations altered, society adapted. This is most evident in "annuals" in particular. Annuals provide us with a yearly record of the changes over time in literature. They may provide some answers but possibly raise even more questions, including whether the content selection was about informing people or conforming the public.

<u>**What are Annuals?**</u>

Publishers from around the1820s in Britain and 1850 in Australia began to produce books known later as annuals. These contained short stories, drawings, parts of novels and were directed at families. If a family was only going to buy one book for the year, it soon became an annual. Publishers used it as a form of advertising of books and authors in their stable. It was like a sampler box of chocolates that was used to increase sales. The careful selection of the contents was aimed at aspirational families.

The first British 'annual' was called Forget-Me-Not and it came out in 1823. Surprisingly it was targeting an educated female audience of upper class and upper middle class wealthier members of society. It was full of short stories, poetry, and drawings. It was published through until 1847 and its editions contained the works of famous authors and poets. Its success triggered the publication of many other annuals, rising as high as sixty one titles in 1828 that sold over 100,000 copies. The surge diminished quickly and by 1850 very few remained. Annuals however gained a second wind towards the end of the nineteenth century especially when the target audience was children. This is when the separate titles for each gender took a strong foothold. The Boy's Own Annual (1879) full of adventure stories for boys and The Girl's Own Annual (1880) full of "educational articles" for girls, set the tone for annuals that would follow all the way through to the 1960s.

From a publisher's perspective annuals were a major marketing tool. They allowed the public to become aware of the breadth of authors under the publisher's banner. They gave a foretaste of what was to come the following year and also what may have been missed during the previous year. Other businesses in later years would advertise in them and thus the actual cost of publishing them and marketing them was reduced or became negligible. Publishers also found them to be good vehicles to promote up and coming authors. They would surround these new author's stories with ones by high profile authors and thus ease new authors into the market place.

For authors, the annual became an opportunity to have a small section of an unknown work published. It allowed them to trial a chapter of a story and assess public feedback. Short stories could be published. Annuals also became a small income stream depending on your status. In truth, given the success of the annuals and the binding contracts that publishers had, many authors received no income from them as publishers had enormous power over any content written. Indeed, it wasn't unheard of for some publishers to seek money from authors to have their work included in annuals once annuals became very popular.

The popularity of what initially was a marketing ploy surprised most publishers and, as they became a good revenue source, the quality and therefore the price of them improved. Illustrations, photos, colour plates became features which greatly suited a group of people who often struggled to make ends meet. Artists, illustrators and photographers began to vie with each other to have their work included. In reality they got a pittance for their work but in hard times any income was a relief until they were "discovered".

Purists decried them, but the general reading public lapped them up as annuals offered a broad sample that satisfied various tastes. In fact, as they were released around Christmas time as a teaser for the following year, they became a Christmas present and the release of them by publishers and unwrapping of them on Christmas morning became a Christmas tradition. A tradition that was heavily marketed by publishers.

The rise in educational standards for both genders brought a broader market for them, almost too broad for one book. Publishers, always after new revenue, decided to cater for the wider market by splitting annuals into various categories. Adult and child versions were released and soon after, different ones separately targeting boys and girls became the norm. These books for young boys and girls contained traditional stereotypes.

The selection of material for annuals became more and more refined. Often annuals were the main purchase for a family and became a joint Christmas present able to be read and enjoyed by people with different interests. The splitting of the types of annuals by gender made sure that households with a predominantly male or female make-up would be catered for and perhaps even one of each gender-oriented book might be purchased in mixed gendered households. It was also important that adults would enjoy the book as well as they were the ones actually buying it. Male adults would be able to pretend that they were reliving parts of their youth in the derring-do adventures. Female adults were able to look back at the friendships and sophistication that they probably wished they had in their youth. All of this made not only the books popular and the publication house more profitable, it helped reinforce the socially expected and accepted roles of both genders. For males there was the touch of exotic places to lure them in. For females in a very class ridden society, an illusion of the way the wealthy and elite lived was painted for them.

The timing of the release of annuals was critical as far as publishers were concerned. Christmas as previously mentioned, was a time when even the poorest of people tried to spend more frivolously. By buying a book that the whole family could enjoy over the next twelve months or more, lower middle-class to upper middle-class families could see value for money. Books represented sophistication and were seen as signs that you were moving onwards and upwards. The publishing houses not only could smell the pudding at Christmas; they could smell the money coming in from the sale of annuals. The books themselves may have cost a fraction more to produce, but that was more than compensated by:

a) the lack of need for marketing as the books sold themselves,

b) a much broader market,

c) the knowledge that the books looked very expensive.

If you throw in the fact that they were like what we have come to know as trailers for movies, they were actually a lure to members of the public to buy books in the following year. Contributors were often people trying to make a name for themselves or maintain that name in public purview. The cost to the publishers for the work was minimal especially as the stories were short, or they had the author within their fold already.

The pictures both drawn and painted reinforced the type of society that was the ideal. There were large colour plates that were painted and then printed in each book. However, the consistent colour of skin was white in all the main characters. The few people of different colour in annuals were depicted as poor, uneducated and often in servitude. Society was not only being kept ignorant of the real world, but cultural, ethnic and gender stereotypes were thrust upon it. It could be done readily because the vast majority of the content in annuals was fiction. Anyone who dared to complain would be confronted with the argument that the writers were using their poetic licence in representing characters, plots and situations. Were they expressing commonly accepted norms of the time, or pursuing an agenda of reinforcing the class and gender bias that upper class males desired? Annuals certainly were an excellent vehicle for the latter as they became quite popular in mid to late Victorian times especially in Britain which was a bastion of such prejudices in that period.

The Content of Annuals

The subject matter in children's annuals changed as technology and world events changed. For boys there was a steady diet of cars, car racing and car chases, along with planes boats and later space ships. Girls saw little variation however. Horses, relationships, school and family were their common fare. It appeared that for them at least that it may have been to show them their place in the world, or because publishers didn't understand what girls were really interested in. Surprisingly the recessions of the 1890s and 1900s and even the Great Depression of 1929-1939 had no impact on annuals. The roaring twenties did, as did any upswing in the economy. It appeared that the publishers of annuals were giving the government line that all was well.

The authors chosen to have their work published in annuals had a very formulaic writing style. But then again, it was difficult to paint a very complex scene in just a few pages, the more so for girls it seems as the settings and props for boys came from the subject matter.

Some authors gained notoriety and their starts from having very short stories published in annuals; others kept their names in the public eye with these stories. How many authors were rejected or deliberately chose not to use this media is unknown. Of the latter, how many did it on principle, and how many because their writing style made it difficult, too is unknown. However, the final say rested with the publishers who seemed to have no qualms about plagiarism and plot stealing which is obvious when imitations of stories and writing styles of well-known authors appeared in shortened versions inside annuals. Lip service appeared to be paid to the Berne Convention signed in 1886 on copyright. Indeed, that convention had to be continually revised as authors and publishers found loopholes to exploit. However, authors such as Captain W.E. Johns of Biggles fame and Enid Blyton contributed under their own names to annuals and thus publishers used their names as marketing tools. All through this time period there was a massive increase in technological development. The use of electricity, phones, motor vehicles and planes were just some of these. They appeared however mainly in boys' annuals which further entrenched the notion that men were the great inventors and only they knew how things worked. The annuals therefore portrayed a range of careers for men and very few for women. Women were homemakers, teachers, clerical workers or nurses. That perception from a male dominated society and supported by books such as annuals, stifled opportunities for women, relegated them down the list of potential employees in most industries, and curtailed academic opportunities.

Following the second world war, females were portrayed as having few aspirations beyond having the latest labour-saving devices in their house, in particular their kitchen which was their domain. They were expected to be well dressed, well-mannered and deferential to males. This role modelling was predominant all through the 1950s and early 1960s and was at its most blatant in children's annuals which focused on the perfect family homes.

<u>**Stereotyping - Class system**</u>

When education of the middle class and the lower class was being brought in, books were the fodder for that learning. The trade-off for that education was a diet of books that reinforced the status quo. The characters in the books in most cases did not represent the majority of people, particularly the conditions that they lived under. Language in the books was more refined and activities were those that the upper middle class and upper class were primarily involved in.

In Victorian England, class levels had to be maintained and people were not encouraged to rise above their station as that had political and economic consequences. To a poor family who saw education and in particular reading as a means for their children to live a better life, books were gold. Anything in them was seen to be true. In Australia there was a hidden class system. There were landowners and renters, wealthy business operators and workers. There may not have been the tugging of forelocks in Australia but every poor person and worker knew where they stood.

There are many people who are involved in the production and selection of material for annuals and each person has their own conscious or unconscious bias that gets added to the mix. From the author, to the editor and on to the publisher, each has a say in the material that makes it into these popular books. Few books were banned outright in the late Victorian period but many authors found that conforming was the only way to get published. Pressure was put on publishers from many quarters but predominantly by prudish, but very influential members of mainly high society. These people had expectations that had to be met and many publishers who relied on patronage, financial support in difficult times and good publicity, could not afford to contravene unwritten biases of these people. As a result, criticism of affluent society or the oppression of the poor and working class never really entered mainstream publications. Publishers knew which side their bread was buttered and even told what brand of butter they had to use. Publishers leant on editors and editors leant on authors. Self-publishing by authors rang a death knell for their career. Consequently, they wrote within certain constraints and the depiction of people in stories was formulated along the lines of the most influential of society. Nowhere was this more apparent than in what was selected for annuals, particularly for children's annuals. Children were exposed through literature to a certain preconceived view of what a society was. They probably found that it was nothing like the one they lived in, but it was one they were subtly taught to aspire to. They had presented to them heroes who always were male, handsome and always won. Women were on the periphery and subordinate to males even in girls' annuals in many cases. Roles weren't explicitly set out, but were preset.

Stereotyping - Gender

The most obvious area of influence was in the stereotyping of genders. But were the publishers merely reflecting society or was there an ulterior motive? Were they trying to keep the status quo on the status of women in society and the presumed superiority of men? Such superiority harked back to the caveman days where women were gatherers of food and mothers, and men were hunters and defenders. There were some very significant periods in the late nineteenth and early twentieth centuries where the roles of women came very much into question. For many centuries women were treated as little more than chattels by men. They were breeding machines, house keepers and expected to satisfy men's desires. Payment for women was a roof over their head, clothes and food. They were little more than slaves.

The industrial revolution changed that somewhat and work from factories was outsourced often to women, who, though they had to hand over their earnings to their husband, began to see that there was more to life than being house bound. Although the industrial revolution impacted the employment of men, many of whom lost jobs; to some extent it benefited women who were in demand because employers could pay them at a lesser rate than men. Women began to have more feelings of self-worth that was actually measurable in monetary terms for the first time, even though they weren't allowed to keep it. It was well-known (albeit a fallacy) that women didn't understand money. The truth was that they did. They had managed to feed and clothe their families on a pittance that their husbands reluctantly gave them. Employers saw the need to train their employees, understanding that an educated workforce was worth the investment. Formal education for women and girls, which for years was only the province of males and very wealthy females, began to make its way down the social ladder.

At a time of the suffragette movement, publishers continued to publish material that depicted women in traditional roles. Nowhere is this more evident than in the books that became known as annuals. Women were depicted as weak, ignorant and demure. Men were always shown to be strong, intelligent and very outgoing. The suffragette movement was strong in England, the US and Australia at the turn of the 1900s, yet equality of women was barely mentioned in annuals.

A more educated group of women had its drawbacks for men, as the rights of women were raised and questioned by women, to such an extent that there was even a push by women to have the right to vote. This women's rights movement was one of the first significant periods where the roles of women were questioned. Publishers suddenly had a new market that they wanted to exploit. However, they also had to deal with the backlash by mainly educated males who were not impressed with any narratives that cast women in a different light other than what had been the norm for hundreds of years. It depended on the publisher as to how far the boundaries could be pushed.

Publishers were responding more to sales and at last women writers began to have their works printed. As a salve to the social mores of what has become known as the Victorian period, there was the beginning of books tailored for girls and others tailored for boys. They reflected what society expected of both genders. Boys were presented as headstrong intelligent active and brave. Girls were shown to be attractive, a bit ditzy and interested in more mundane things and definitely not in women's rights. The annuals, which were collections of stories and poems were perfect examples of this gender division and role parameters that were put in place by a patriarchal society that was unwilling to accept change.

Women and girls towards the second half of each of the World Wars in the twentieth century were being recruited to take on farmwork or factory work which were the traditional roles of men who were now on the battlefields fighting or under the battlefields buried. In the war itself as shown in stories in annuals, men were the heroes and women played second fiddle as nurses nowhere near the battlefields, or they were seen to be trying to do the work of men and somehow remaining elegantly dressed and maintaining a household with the assistance of servants. Women were portrayed in annuals at this time as something different from the vacuous clothes-horses of earlier and later years. Particularly in girls' annuals in the hardest times during these wars, girls and women's stories showed women with resolve and capable of doing almost anything a man could do. Perhaps these were the best times where gender stereotyping was set aside.

Within two years following these major wars and the flu pandemic of 1919, the gender stereotyping was back to status quo. Yearly annuals, particularly ones in a series, distinctly show the roller-coaster ride that equality between genders was on. Men and boys remained constant. They were depicted as strong, loud, decisive, intelligent and up for a fight. Women and girls, depending on major social and economic events, in the main were portrayed as the opposite. In fact, their characters lacked substance by comparison to males even in girls' annuals.

Boys were depicted as young brave men fighting pretend battles and uncovering spy networks. Girls changed little in the stories in annuals, although in the segregated annuals (boy/girl) they began to be depicted as more intelligent.

Following each of the wars, the reality was that the men who survived took back their old jobs and women were back at home. This didn't help the women who were the only breadwinner in the family. There wasn't any mention of post-traumatic stress in annuals. People appeared to go back exactly to the way they were living prior to the war. Whether that was a direct intention of publishers or not is debatable, but while the world was rebuilding after these major wars, in annuals there appeared to be no need for a rebuild. During the darker times of these wars, the annuals tended to put a positive spin on things almost as if they were part of the recruiting process.

The same sort of thing was happening in the new media of cinematography and so readers of annuals were getting confirmation from another source that was at odds with reality. Women were portrayed as simple indolent creatures who needed the protection of men. This new 'reality' was at odds with the reality of people's day to day lives. Whether that led to books and movies as escapism or made people think that they were somehow living their life wrong, or it was an aspirational lifestyle being presented, is not known.

The true situation after the First World War was that because the soldier attrition was so high, some women were forced into remaining in many previously male-dominated vocations. Fathers, brothers and sons had been sacrificed at a horrific rate. To support themselves and their families, women were retrained and sent to work in factories on less pay than their male counterparts. To most males, it was eye-opening what women could do. It came as no surprise to women though. Many employers found that they lost some of their best workers in this push back to normality. There was a lot of resistance and dissatisfaction expressed by women who had stepped in and done the hard yards in a time of crisis. Publishers glossed over the fact that women had proved their worth and had also gained greater self-esteem and self-awareness. What they had been taught to be and what was deemed 'normal' in published works, many women found to be out of touch with reality.

Publishers once again tried to also toe the social line and again went back to printing material that tried to reset traditional roles. Annuals produced during this post war period reflected what the expectations were. Brave fearless men and simpering dependent women became the literary fodder that hit bookshops, libraries and schools. Scripts in the quickly developing movie industry reinforced those traditional roles. Many early films had major roles for men and some bit parts for women, ones that in today's terms would be called eye candy. A lot of the early films were based on historical events which compounded the issue as history was written by men about men. Often annuals during this period contained stories that might end up as films or were stories based on film scripts.

The division of gender and specific gender roles were very strong in literature during the 1920s and 1930s. Whether that was a push by governments, whether it came from males wishing to reassert their dominance, or whether it was a cry from the majority of society wanting to desperately go back to a time that was before the horrors of the First World War, is hard to know. It could be a combination of all these and others. However, judging just by the annuals published during this period, something was driving this reverting back to the very traditional roles. Were publishers complicit in the push? Were they the actual drivers of the push? Or were they just out to cash in? The printed works, particularly those targeting children and teenagers, definitely reflect the reverting back to quieter, more socially constrained times. The illustrations including the colour plates reinforce the roles of genders.

There was a marked trend post-World War two for product placement in teenage annuals although not very blatant, in children's annuals. This product placement included toys and sporting equipment, clothes and even food. In particular clothing fashion appears to be more high-end and for women points more to upcoming fashion trends rather than current or past trends. Perhaps this points to the fact that publishers and in particular, editors, were probably able make money from advertisers who would use annuals as influencers. This was most evident in the radio show annuals and later movie annuals that were produced in the twentieth century. If advertisers were able to have a say in the content of annuals, who else could? Conservative groups probably became aware that this medium was reaching so many households and now had another means of communicating their message. Associations such as youth groups and religious groups also began using their own annuals to push their own agendas. These groups had less success when publishers produced annuals based on the growing number of television shows during the 1950s and 1960s. More traditional annuals could not compete with the stylised ones that had easily recognisable characters and were produced by television shows. Annuals became just part of the general merchandise for a TV production company. As TV shows of that period still pushed gender stereotypes, nothing much changed except the quality of literature which took a nose-dive.

Across the decades, annuals tended to reflect social mores and values of previous generations as the content was heavily focused on times that appeared better than what was being experienced. This changed somewhat during the 1950s and 1960s when younger people had more money and that meant they wanted content they could better relate to. The scientific advances during this period were huge and the content had to change to reflect a more modern society. However, behind the cosmetic changes the message being peddled didn't change much at all. Women were still being portrayed as somewhat lesser than men. They may have looked and sounded more educated and sophisticated but the male was the dominant person, the breadwinner and decision maker even in some of the annuals targeted for girls.

Stereotyping - Racism and the British Bias

Gender bias was endemic and racism was too. This was the society that publishers decided to present to the public and demand authors write about. The Australian Annuals were very much carbon copies of what was being served up in Britain. In fact, a number of publishers would market the British versions in Australia or just alter some of the content to give it an Australian flavour. There would be the occasional Australian story, quiz, crossword puzzle or reference made to Australian events slotted in amongst the very heavily slanted British material. What was seen as de rigueur and the status quo in Britain was what was portrayed in Australian annuals. Boarding schools were seen to be common to both countries, whereas they were not. Boarding schools were generally for the wealthy in Australia. The British class system was at odds with what was perceived to be the way of Australians. There was a class system in Australia but not as overt as the British one. Two things were common though and that was the racism and the misogynism. People with different skin colour were seen to be poorly educated, have unacceptable ways of behaving and were expected to be subjugated by their Anglo-Saxon superiors. This applied to Australian first nation people more so than anyone else. It wasn't subtly expressed in stories and illustrations, it was blatant.

The one glaring aspect of annuals that went against the notion that the annuals reflected the situation around them, was the way British influence remained very high even as the empire/commonwealth declined. Whilst one would not expect that the geopolitical situation would be a focus in children's annuals, there was an undertone in both British and Australian books that Britain was still the major power even up until the 1950s. To Australian children even in the 1960s, England was still the mother country and Australia was still a backwater with little history and little culture. The selection of articles, short stories and illustrations reflected this. London was the centre of the universe and English schools and universities provided the best education. Morals and standards were British and the royal family were to be revered. Historical stories in annuals were inevitably British and involved British victories. As British colonial rule waned and independence was sought by countries after each of the World Wars, Australian annuals didn't reflect this. On the contrary, there appears to have been a push to reinforce that there was no change happening at all. The Australian identity was being quashed or continued to be identified as lacking in culture, refinement and substance.

As colonial rule declined, the portrayal of those from different cultures as often ignorant or evil increased. Children were being exposed to racism from an early age. The Boxer Rebellion at the beginning of the twentieth century cast the Chinese into an even worse light than before. In Africa, any battle by any aspiring nation, even if it was lost by the British was shown as a positive moral and righteous victory of English character. Children were fed on a diet of bravery of soldiers, guaranteed victory against evil hordes in far flung lands by a superior British force. This was shown in many genres, even down to crossword clues.

And when there was a need to break away from this British history model, for boys, the wild west of the USA was added to the menu. First nation people were cast as ignorant savages not as people defending their lands against invaders. The lawlessness depicted was met with force of the cowboy hero and justice was dispensed at the end of a gun. There was a period after the first world war and all the way through second world war and up until the 1950s where many boys' annuals had one or more stories about the wild west. These reinforced the gun culture, the idea that heroes never die, the idea that white males were stronger and better than anyone else, that women were merely decorative and that people who looked different were less than human. For children at the time, children who were unable or not well versed in the capacity to tell fact from fiction, their concept of the world, their establishing of a sense of values, is likely to have been severely impacted by what they were exposed to in the literature, including children's annuals, that they read or had read to them.

Far off exotic places as depicted in annuals and other literature became their geography lessons; British history became their history; biased views and representations of other cultures became their social sciences; and as for science and logic, religion, particularly Christianity in the early parts of the twentieth century, was put forward in many annuals as truths to mask such things as Darwinism.

<u>Stereotyping - Religion</u>

The idea that there was only one true religion, and that being Christianity, permeated a lot of articles and stories in children's annuals. Children learned words such as heathen and pagan early on as they were ascribed to anything non-Christian. Stories of the bravery of the knights of the crusade trying to rescue Jerusalem from the Saracens failed to mention that the Saracens were the people who lived there and that Jerusalem was seen as a holy city for many religions. Nor did they mention how such a religious "adventure" cost the people back in European and British countries heavily in taxes, because war is an expensive business.

Despite the atrocities including cannibalism and attacks on Jews back in their own countries, the crusaders were portrayed as being righteous defenders of religion in the stories in children's annuals thus raising Christianity above all other religions in the eyes of young children. They were being taught this in church and at school, and were having it reinforced through what they read.

Publishers' Role

Publishers are able to frame the content that the fertile active minds of young children. What they choose to publish in books including annuals has a great impact on what a child will believe. What someone learns as a "fact" in their childhood is very difficult to contradict when they are older. Publishers are in a unique position akin to that of the clergy, teachers, parents and media content decision makers. But who are publishers answerable to? Who and what influences their decisions as to what should and shouldn't be published, and why? Sales of books determine many of those decisions, particularly these days.

With the establishment of schools for all children and compulsory education in Britain in 1870 and Australia in 1872, publishers particularly of prescribed textbooks had a virtual monopoly on what children were exposed to. Censorship was rife, not just on terms of sexually explicit content but in other aspects such as religious, political and even at times scientific information. That censorship was not just by governments but by publishers themselves who had their own sets of values they wished to adhere to. It was a powerful position to be in.

Authors were seeking to have their books published. Organisations were seeking to have their own particular views published. Were the publishers through the years entirely independent? As long as money was involved, it seems unlikely. Annuals were seen as a good way to test the waters. They brought in revenue from advertising. They offered opportunities to publishers to find out whether an author, a genre, a subject matter, a viewpoint would be worth pursuing in the following year. There was a ready market for these samplers. Did people pay to have their work or their viewpoint published? It was also all about product placement in later years. Above all publishers were businessmen (and they were nearly all men) and they were only in it to make money. However, they were in a privileged position and a powerful one. Publishers long ago and to a lesser extent now, were the decision makers of radio and TV of the later modern world. They were the gatekeepers at the portal of what people were exposed to in terms of their knowledge.

Framing Society

In discussing the possibilities that publishers may have other motivations apart from money when it came to publishing material in annuals, much of it is conjecture. That being said, the evidence of what was being published year upon year in annuals does indicate that careful selection of material took place and most of this reflected a stereotyping of people who were not male, not Christian, not fitting the traditional European image and were not of the middle to upper middle class. The question that arises is who gains from all of this?

Governments wishing the status quo to be retained which meant that wealthy white men heavily influenced the direction of a country. Banks and other lending institutions would have a ready long-term market as people were wanting to move up through the class system. Private schools, clothing manufacturers and even toy and sporting companies benefited. Christian churches also did too as they were depicted as part of a normal and important part of everyday life. It could be said that everyone benefited as an aspirational society drove an economy. However, the narrow focus of nearly all literature as evidenced by these chocolate box samplers, the annuals, perhaps stifled creative literature. In much the same way as artists painted commercial works of art to get by, authors had to, as well.

Subliminally, conservative thinkers were able to push others into being conservative. Class levels were reaffirmed and gender roles remained as they were. Children's annuals were big sellers and to have these effectively censored meant that children were trained to know their place. Unsurprisingly annuals didn't contain new radical ideas especially those of feminism and of the suffragette movement. To even hint at that, meant publishers would have their livelihood threatened. Money was everything and those with it controlled everything. The status quo had to be maintained in everything and that fed into literature. Even excellent quality literature at the time suffered and many great authors struggled.

We look back now and possibly can't believe the narrow parameters that authors, editors and publishers had to abide by. However, sales were determined by public opinion and that opinion was controlled by a minority of influential people. Tracking the actual lifestyles of different eras cannot be accurately done by looking at annuals for this very reason. You can track the type of society that the wealthy wanted. You can track the prudishness of a time and the censorship that was applied. You can track the stereotyping, gender expectations and racism over the years, but you will not get a good idea of what society was really like particularly for the middle, lower and poor classes.

<u>**Conclusion**</u>

There is evidence to put forward a case that stereotyping people took place in literature from 1850 through to the late 1960s. The changes in the content in annuals in that period suggests that publishers played a role in that stereotyping. And it is this racial and gender and other stereotyping that perhaps leads to the questioning of a hidden purpose in this style of literature. As the world was opening up and women in particular were becoming better educated, the very paternalistic male dominated people in power may have wanted to retain the status quo. Reinforcing that through literature was not something new. Targeting young minds with suitable role models had always occurred but as now boys and girls were receiving an education, another avenue had opened up for it and allowed the creating of more bias and conformity. In fact, these things were needed. Free thinking was deemed dangerous by conservatives,

The use of literature and motion pictures to promote a social model or a particular action was even more carefully crafted. During wars, patriotism was played upon to boost numbers on the battlefield. During the Great Depression there was a sense of normality portrayed even though nothing was normal. A close analysis of annuals during these world events shows that positive aspirational spin being put on bleak political messages, or there was an escapism into a fantasy world on offer as an alternative to reality.

There is no definitive proof that publishers and those with money, power and influence conspired to present to young fertile minds.

There is ample evidence that it occurred in Germany in the 1930s and is occurring in many countries these days. The power of the printed word is still enormous. To many people, what they read is still considered gospel truth even though there are counter arguments put forward that disprove what they have read. Between 1850 and the late 1960s as the world became more educated, there weren't the avenues and the voices to argue the case that what was being published was wrong, was propaganda, and benefited conservative beliefs. The subtle direction of thought as shown in annuals during that period quelled and quashed opinions that were contrary to the status quo.

Publishers may not have been the sole arbiters of the content of what was printed for the consumption of others. They had businesses to run and profits to be made. They however had a responsibility for whatever was printed under their name. They would argue that they were just telling life as it was, but were they?